FIRST 50 SONGS

YOU SHOULD PLAY ON SOLO GUITAR

T0079419

ISBN 978-1-5400-4565-2

For all works contained herein:
Unauthorized copying, arranging, adapting, recording, Internet posting, public performance,
or other distribution of the music in this publication is an infringement of copyright.
Infringers are liable under the law.

Visit Hal Leonard Online at
www.halleonard.com

World headquarters, contact:
Hal Leonard
7777 West Bluemound Road
Milwaukee, WI 53213
Email: info@halleonard.com

In Europe, contact:
Hal Leonard Europe Limited
1 Red Place
London, W1K 6PL
Email: info@halleonardeurope.com

In Australia, contact:
Hal Leonard Australia Pty. Ltd.
4 Lentara Court
Cheltenham, Victoria, 3192 Australia
Email: info@halleonard.com.au

GUITAR NOTATION LEGEND

Guitar music can be notated three different ways: on a *musical staff*, in *tablature*, and in *rhythm slashes*.

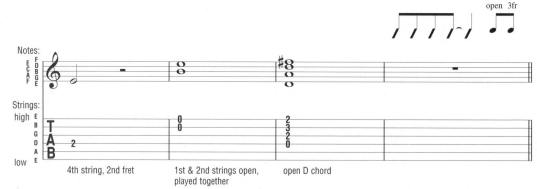

RHYTHM SLASHES are written above the staff. Strum chords in the rhythm indicated. Use the chord diagrams found at the top of the first page of the transcription for the appropriate chord voicings. Round noteheads indicate single notes.

THE MUSICAL STAFF shows pitches and rhythms and is divided by bar lines into measures. Pitches are named after the first seven letters of the alphabet.

TABLATURE graphically represents the guitar fingerboard. Each horizontal line represents a string, and each number represents a fret.

HALF-STEP BEND: Strike the note and bend up 1/2 step.

WHOLE-STEP BEND: Strike the note and bend up one step.

GRACE NOTE BEND: Strike the note and immediately bend up as indicated.

SLIGHT (MICROTONE) BEND: Strike the note and bend up 1/4 step.

BEND AND RELEASE: Strike the note and bend up as indicated, then release back to the original note. Only the first note is struck.

PRE-BEND: Bend the note as indicated, then strike it.

VIBRATO: The string is vibrated by rapidly bending and releasing the note with the fretting hand.

WIDE VIBRATO: The pitch is varied to a greater degree by vibrating with the fretting hand.

HAMMER-ON: Strike the first (lower) note with one finger, then sound the higher note (on the same string) with another finger by fretting it without picking.

PULL-OFF: Place both fingers on the notes to be sounded. Strike the first note and without picking, pull the finger off to sound the second (lower) note.

LEGATO SLIDE: Strike the first note and then slide the same fret-hand finger up or down to the second note. The second note is not struck.

SHIFT SLIDE: Same as legato slide, except the second note is struck.

TRILL: Very rapidly alternate between the notes indicated by continuously hammering on and pulling off.

TAPPING: Hammer ("tap") the fret indicated with the pick-hand index or middle finger and pull off to the note fretted by the fret hand.

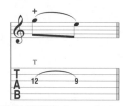

NATURAL HARMONIC: Strike the note while the fret-hand lightly touches the string directly over the fret indicated.

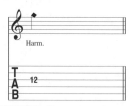

PINCH HARMONIC: The note is fretted normally and a harmonic is produced by adding the edge of the thumb or the tip of the index finger of the pick hand to the normal pick attack.

PICK SCRAPE: The edge of the pick is rubbed down (or up) the string, producing a scratchy sound.

MUFFLED STRINGS: A percussive sound is produced by laying the fret hand across the string(s) without depressing, and striking them with the pick hand.

PALM MUTING: The note is partially muted by the pick hand lightly touching the string(s) just before the bridge.

RAKE: Drag the pick across the strings indicated with a single motion.

TREMOLO PICKING: The note is picked as rapidly and continuously as possible.

VIBRATO BAR DIVE AND RETURN: The pitch of the note or chord is dropped a specified number of steps (in rhythm), then returned to the original pitch.

VIBRATO BAR SCOOP: Depress the bar just before striking the note, then quickly release the bar.

VIBRATO BAR DIP: Strike the note and then immediately drop a specified number of steps, then release back to the original pitch.

CONTENTS

Africa

Words and Music by David Paich and Jeff Porcaro

Copyright © 1982 Hudmar Publishing Co., Inc. and Rising Storm Music
This arrangement Copyright © 2019 Hudmar Publishing Co., Inc. and Rising Storm Music
All Rights for Hudmar Publishing Co., Inc. Controlled and Administered by Spirit Two Music, Inc.
All Rights Reserved   Used by Permission

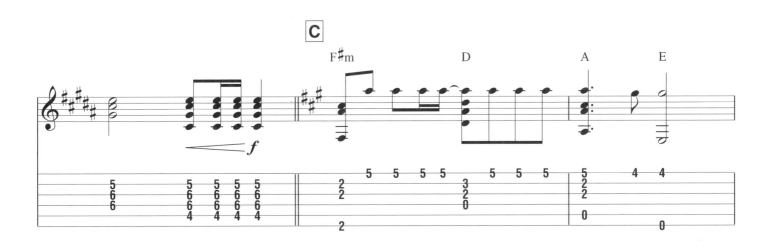

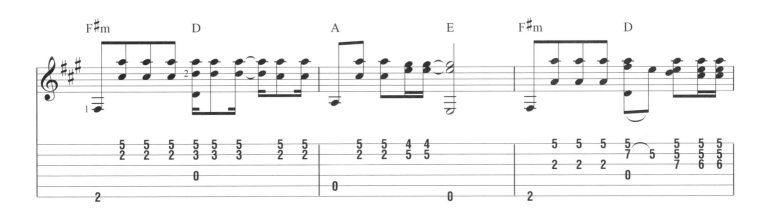

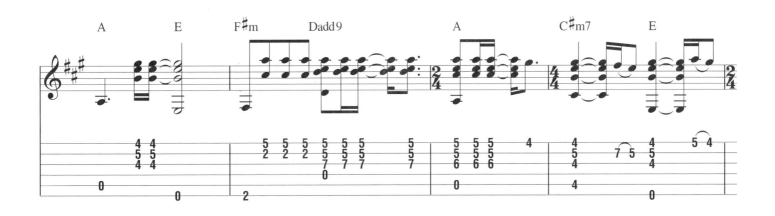

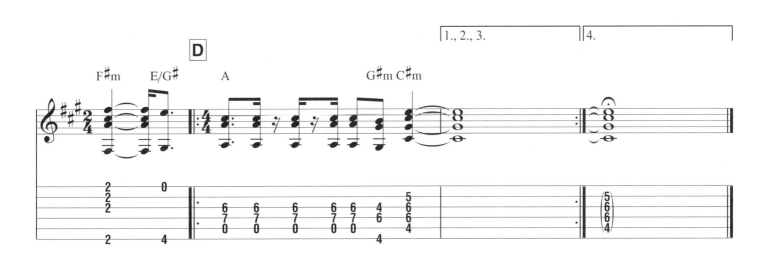

All I Ask of You

from THE PHANTOM OF THE OPERA

Music by Andrew Lloyd Webber
Lyrics by Charles Hart
Additional Lyrics by Richard Stilgoe

Drop D tuning:
(low to high) D-A-D-G-B-E

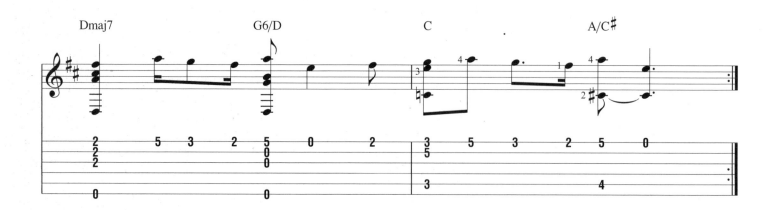

© Copyright 1986 Andrew Lloyd Webber licensed to The Really Useful Group Ltd.
This arrangement © Copyright 2019 Andrew Lloyd Webber licensed to The Really Useful Group Ltd.
International Copyright Secured   All Rights Reserved

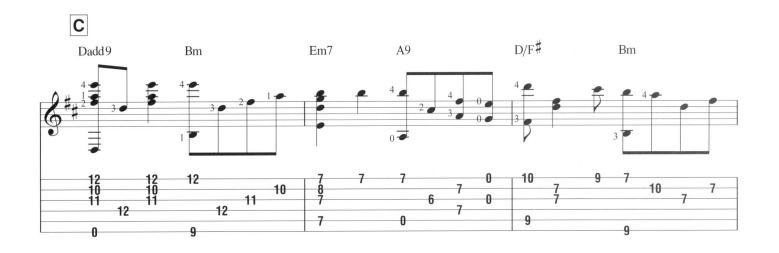

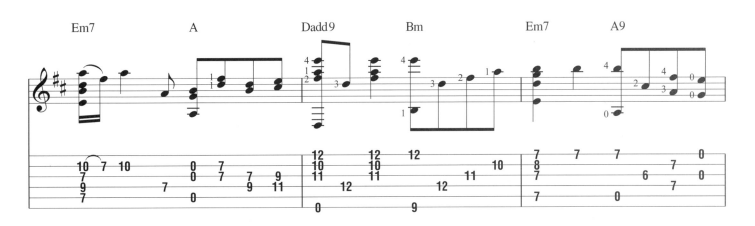

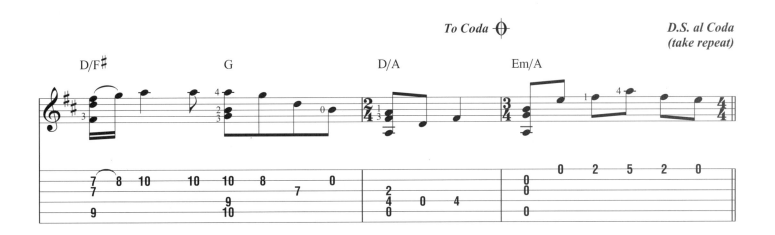

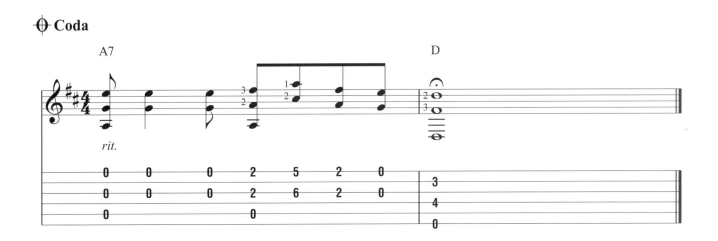

All of Me

Words and Music by John Stephens and Toby Gad

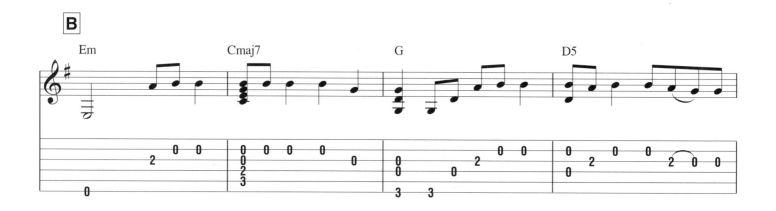

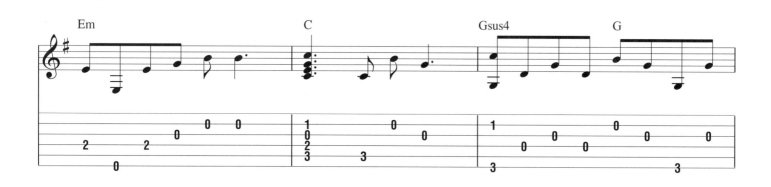

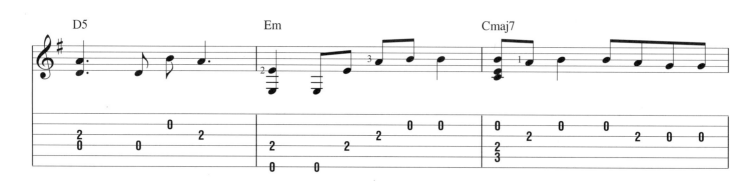

Copyright © 2013 John Legend Publishing, EMI April Music Inc. and Gad Songs, LLC
This arrangement Copyright © 2019 John Legend Publishing, EMI April Music Inc. and Gad Songs, LLC
All Rights for John Legend Publishing Administered by BMG Rights Management (US) LLC
All Rights for EMI April Music Inc. and Gad Songs, LLC Administered by Sony/ATV Music Publishing LLC, 424 Church Street, Suite 1200, Nashville, TN 37219
All Rights Reserved   Used by Permission

Blue Skies

from BETSY

Words and Music by Irving Berlin

© Copyright 1927 by Irving Berlin
Copyright Renewed
This arrangement © Copyright 2007 by the Estate of Irving Berlin
International Copyright Secured   All Rights Reserved

And So It Goes

Words and Music by Billy Joel

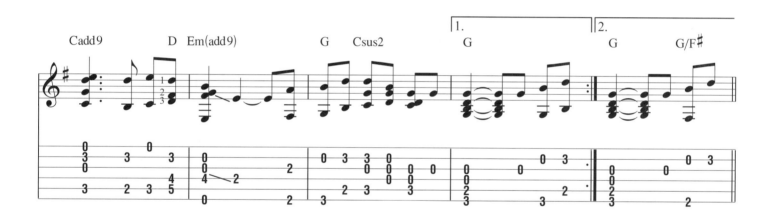

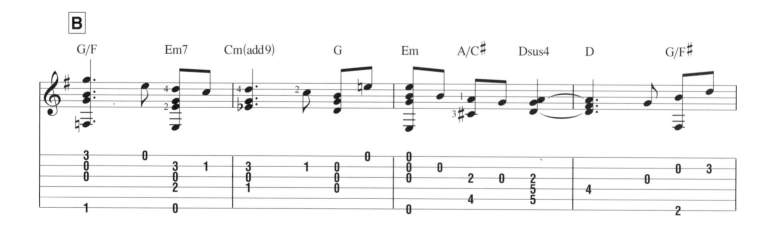

Copyright © 1989 JOELSONGS
This arrangement Copyright © 2019 JOELSONGS
All Rights Administered by ALMO MUSIC CORP.
All Rights Reserved   Used by Permission

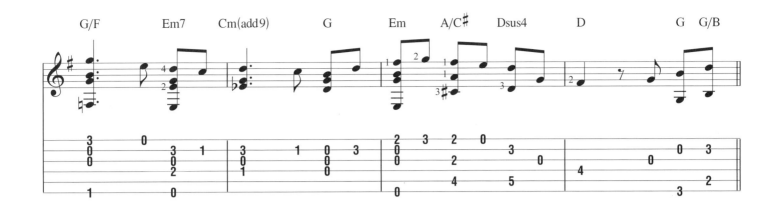

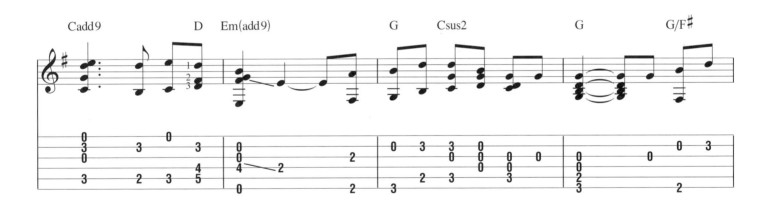

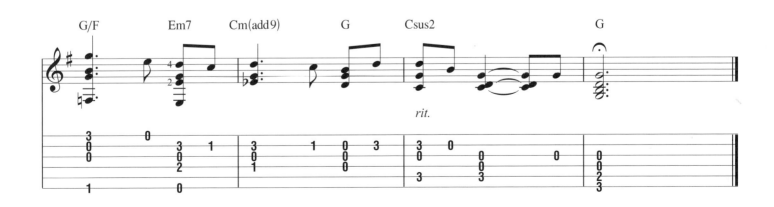

Bésame Mucho
(Kiss Me Much)

Music and Spanish Words by Consuelo Velazquez
English Words by Sunny Skylar

Drop D tuning:
(low to high) D-A-D-G-B-E

Copyright © 1941, 1943 by Promotora Hispano Americana de Musica, S.A.
Copyrights Renewed
This arrangement Copyright © 2019 by Promotora Hispano Americana de Musica, S.A.
All Rights Administered by Peer International Corporation
International Copyright Secured   All Rights Reserved

California Dreamin'

Words and Music by John Phillips and Michelle Phillips

Copyright © 1965 UNIVERSAL MUSIC CORP.
Copyright Renewed
This arrangement Copyright © 2019 UNIVERSAL MUSIC CORP.
All Rights Reserved   Used by Permission

To Coda ⊕

D.S. al Coda

⊕ **Coda**

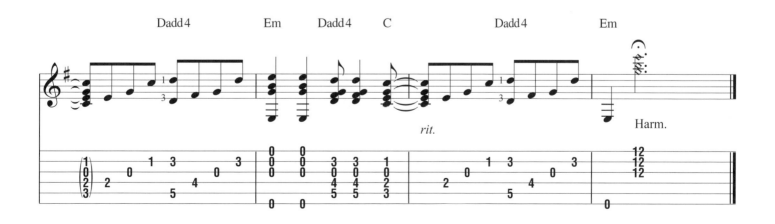

Can't Help Falling in Love

from the Paramount Picture BLUE HAWAII

Words and Music by George David Weiss, Hugo Peretti and Luigi Creatore

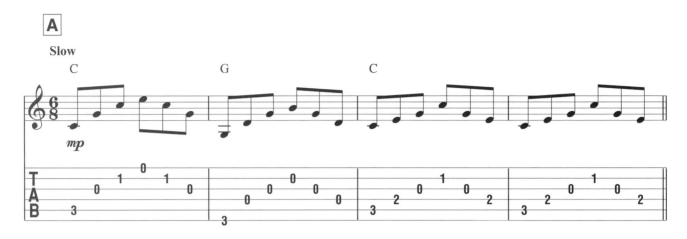

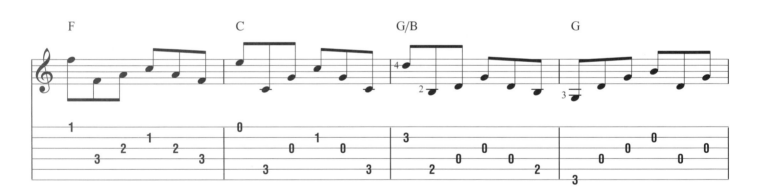

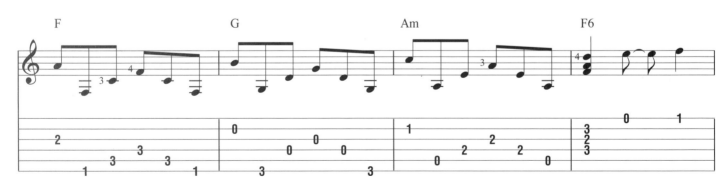

Copyright © 1961 Gladys Music
Copyright Renewed
This arrangement Copyright © 2019 Gladys Music
Extended U.S. Renewal and British Reversionary Territories Assigned to Abilene Music LLC, HJP Music, Hugo Peretti Music and Luigi Creatore Music
Administered in the United States during the Extended Renewal by Steve Peter Music
All Rights Reserved   Used by Permission

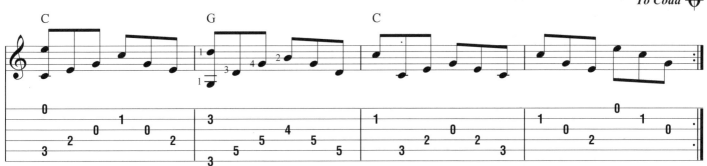

C

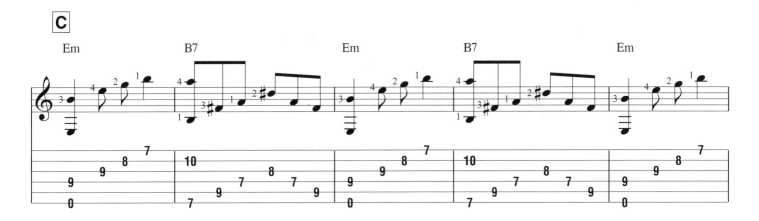

D.S. al Coda
(no repeat)

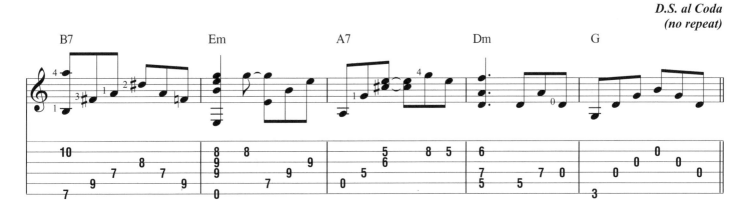

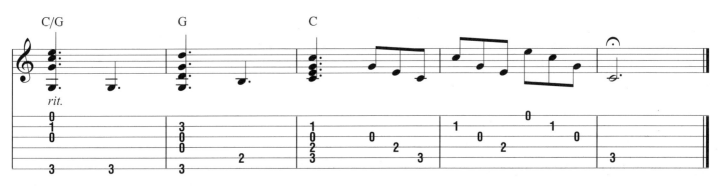

Change the World

Words and Music by Wayne Kirkpatrick, Gordon Kennedy and Tommy Sims

Copyright © 1996 Downtown DMP Songs, Universal - PolyGram International Publishing, Inc., Sondance Kid Music,
Universal Music Corp., Universal Music - Brentwood Benson Publishing and Universal Music - Brentwood Benson Songs
This arrangement Copyright © 2019 Downtown DMP Songs, Universal - PolyGram International Publishing, Inc., Sondance Kid Music,
Universal Music Corp., Universal Music - Brentwood Benson Publishing and Universal Music - Brentwood Benson Songs
All Rights for Downtown DMP Songs Administered by Downtown Music Publishing, LLC
All Rights for Sondance Kid Music Controlled and Administered by Universal - PolyGram International Publishing, Inc.
All Rights for Universal Music - Brentwood Benson Publishing and Universal Music - Brentwood Benson Songs Admin. at CapitolCMGPublishing.com
International Copyright Secured   All Rights Reserved

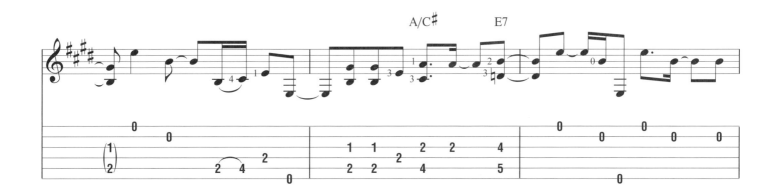

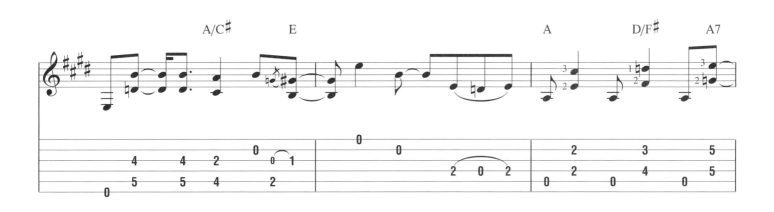

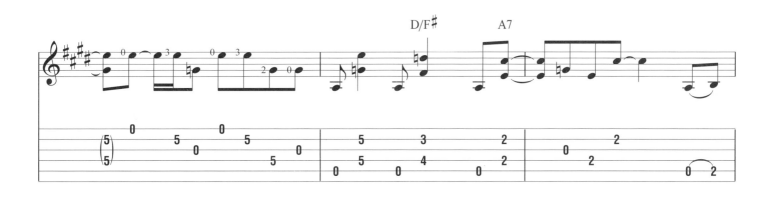

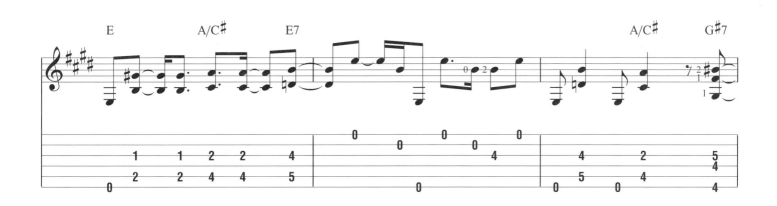

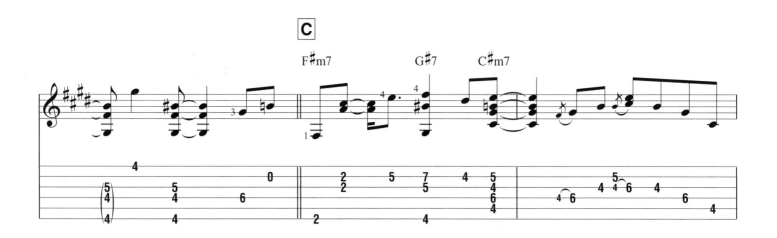

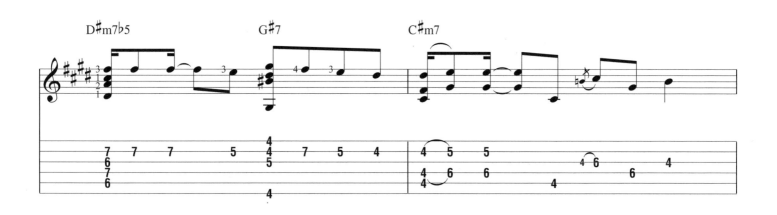

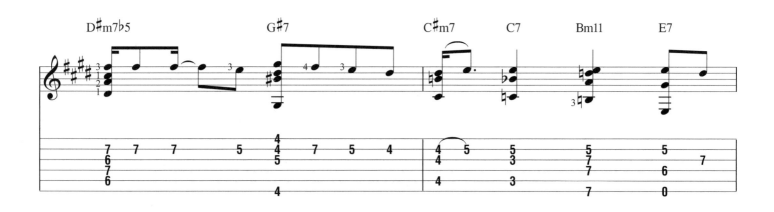

D

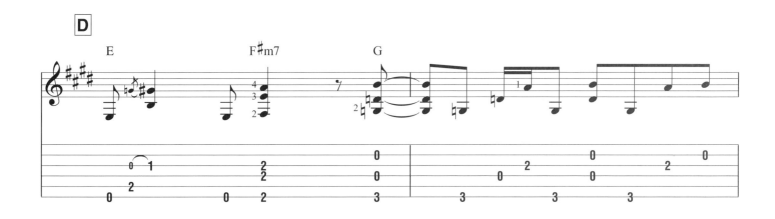

D.S. al Coda

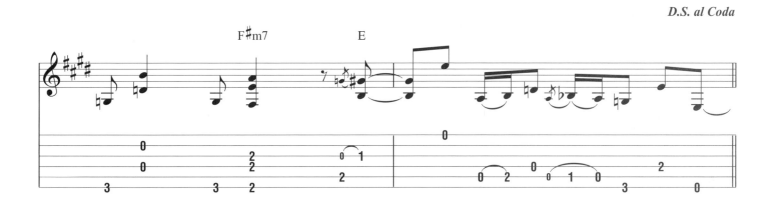

1., 2., 3.

⊕ Coda

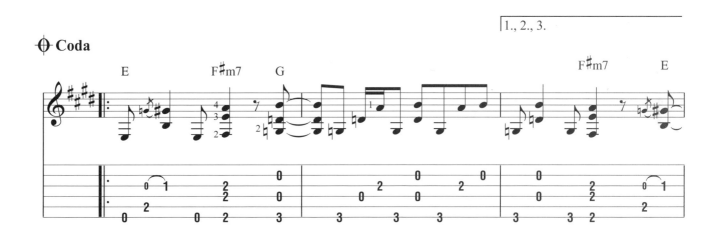

4.

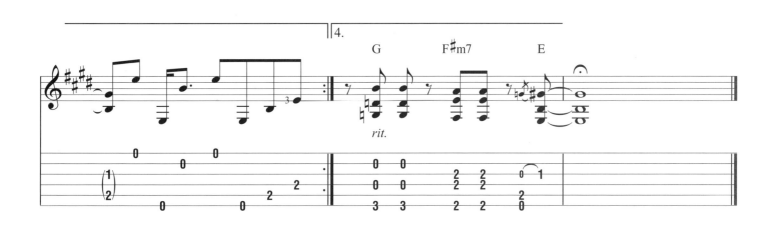

rit.

Cheek to Cheek

from the RKO Radio Motion Picture TOP HAT
Words and Music by Irving Berlin

© Copyright 1935 by Irving Berlin
Copyright Renewed
This arrangement © Copyright 2007 by the Estate of Irving Berlin
International Copyright Secured   All Rights Reserved

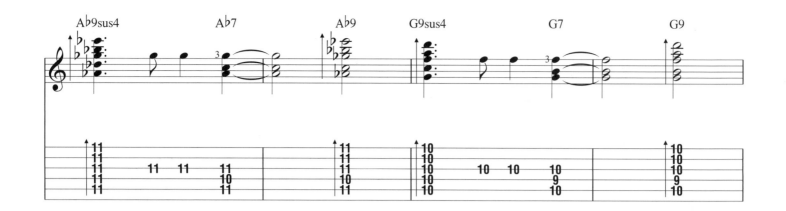

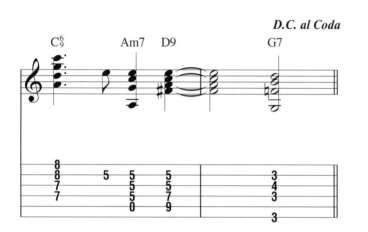

Coda

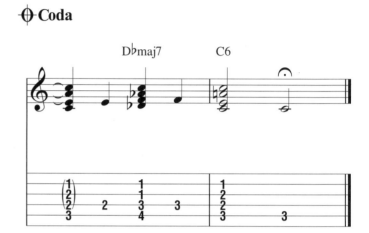

Every Breath You Take

Music and Lyrics by Sting

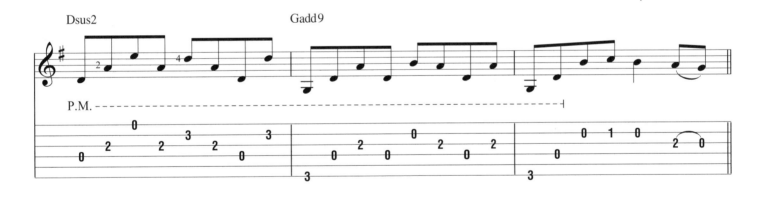

Copyright © 1983 G.M. Sumner
This arrangement Copyright © 2019 G.M. Sumner
All Rights Administered by Sony/ATV Music Publishing LLC, 424 Church Street, Suite 1200, Nashville, TN 37219
International Copyright Secured   All Rights Reserved

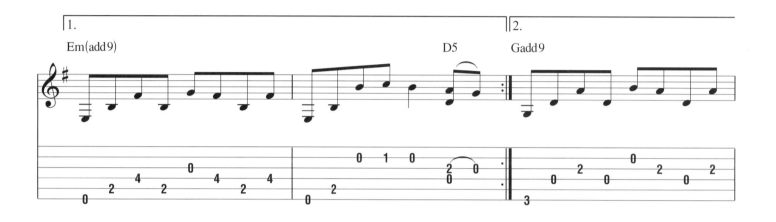

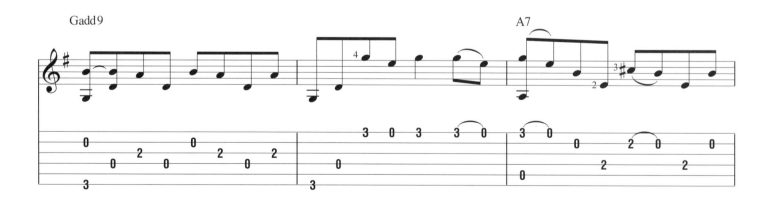

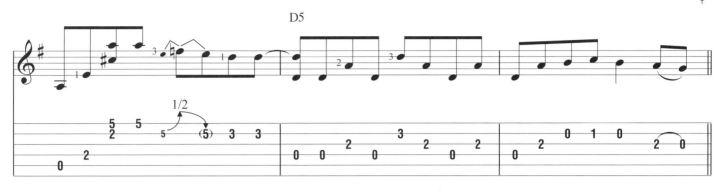

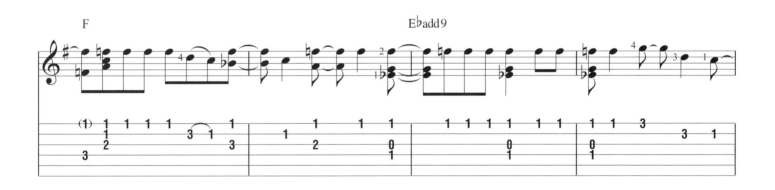

Coda 1

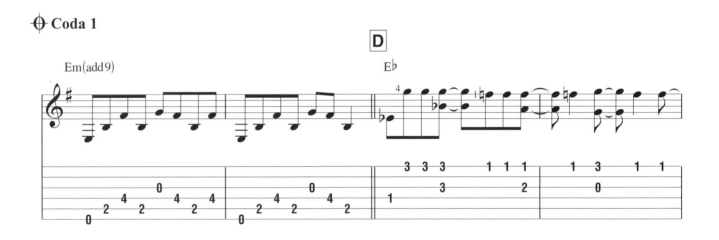

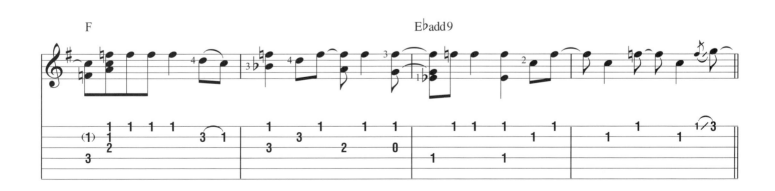

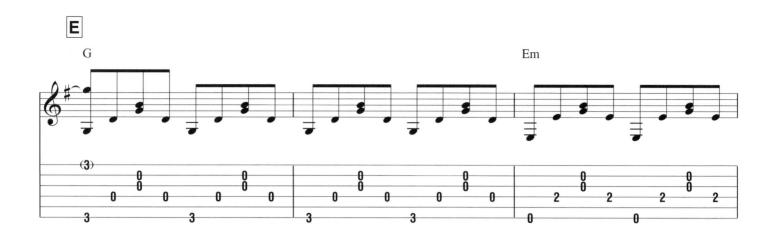

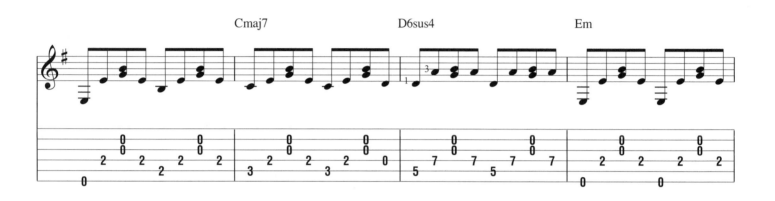

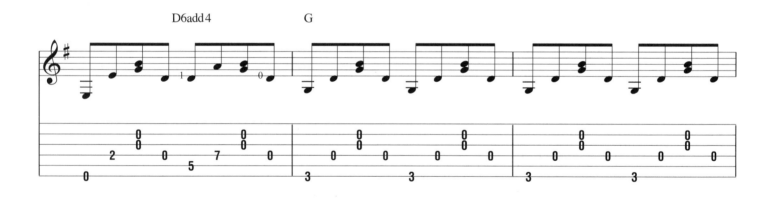

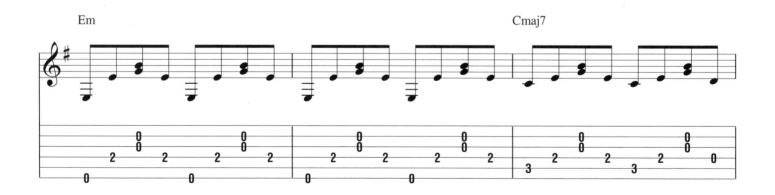

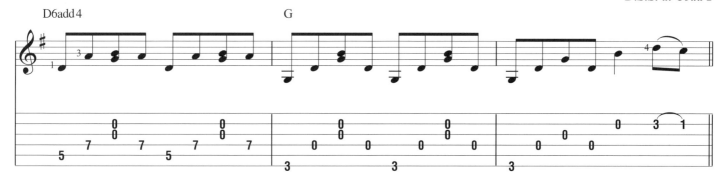

Coda 2

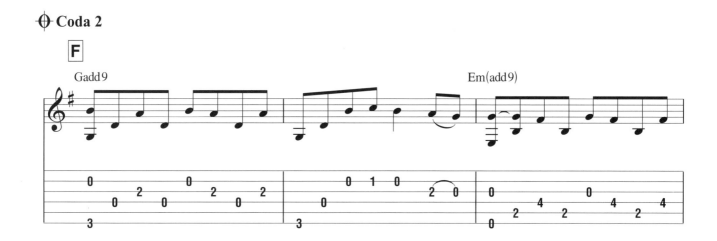

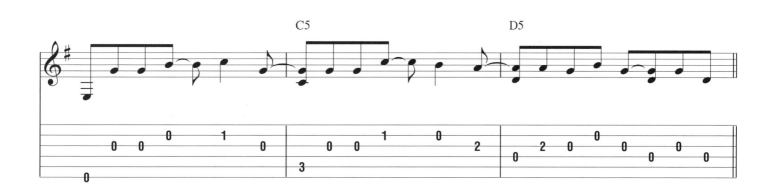

Come Away with Me

Words and Music by Norah Jones

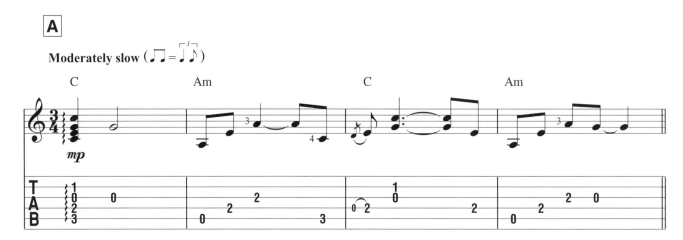

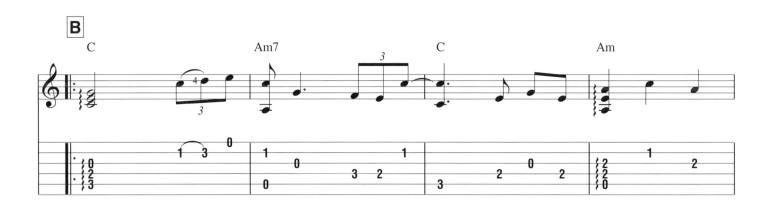

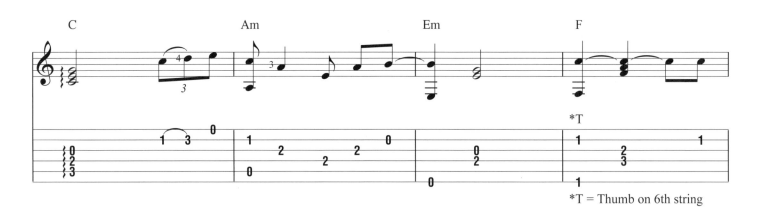

*T = Thumb on 6th string

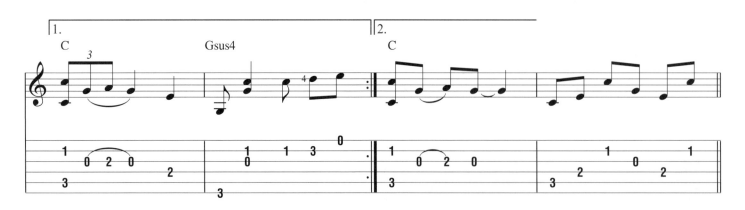

Copyright © 2002 EMI Blackwood Music Inc. and Muthajones Music LLC
This arrangement Copyright © 2019 EMI Blackwood Music Inc. and Muthajones Music LLC
All Rights Administered by Sony/ATV Music Publishing LLC, 424 Church Street, Suite 1200, Nashville, TN 37219
International Copyright Secured   All Rights Reserved

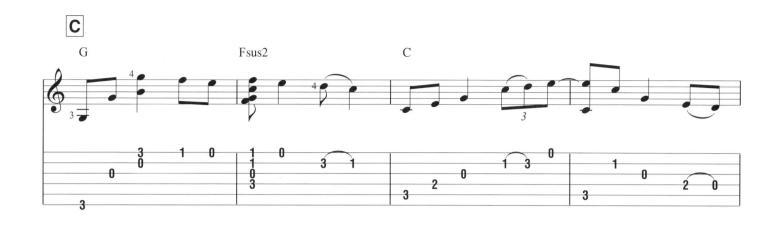

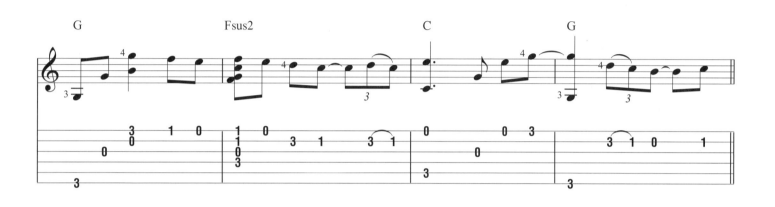

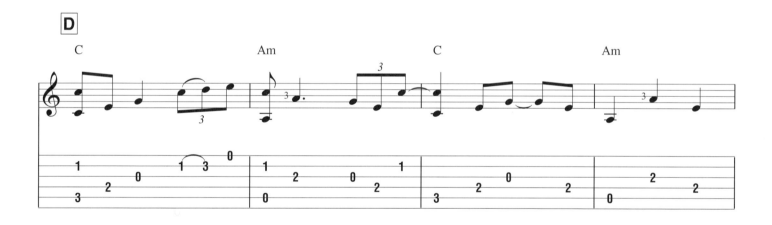

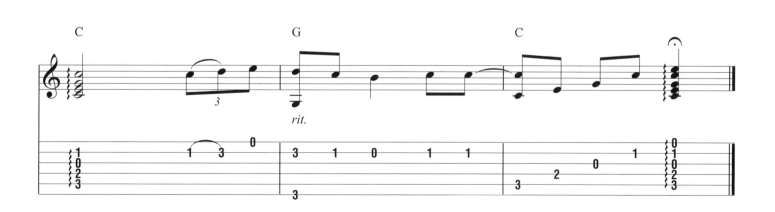

Crazy

Words and Music by Willie Nelson

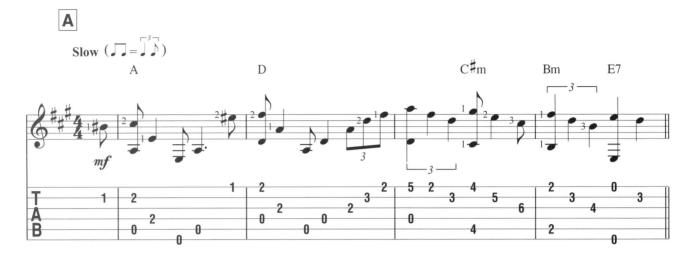

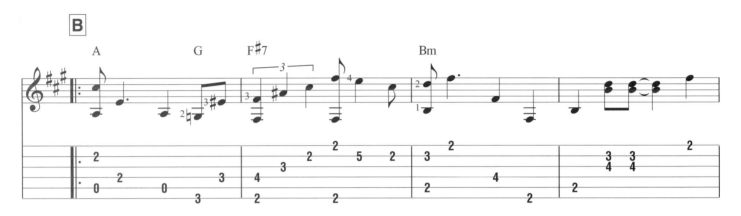

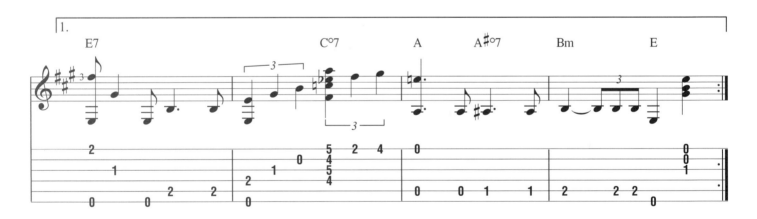

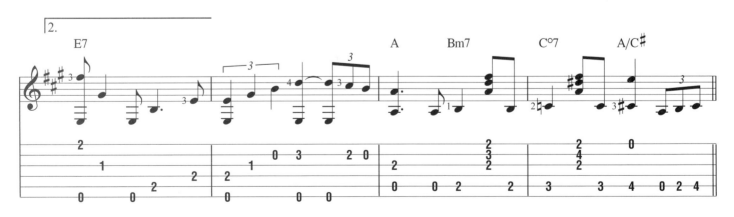

Copyright © 1961 Sony/ATV Music Publishing LLC
Copyright Renewed
This arrangement Copyright © 2019 Sony/ATV Music Publishing LLC
All Rights Administered by Sony/ATV Music Publishing LLC, 424 Church Street, Suite 1200, Nashville, TN 37219
International Copyright Secured   All Rights Reserved

Dream a Little Dream of Me

Words by Gus Kahn
Music by Wilbur Schwandt and Fabian Andree

TRO - © Copyright 1930 (Renewed) and 1931 (Renewed) Essex Music, Inc., Words and Music, Inc., New York, NY,
Don Swan Publications, Miami, FL and Gilbert Keyes Music, Hollywood, CA
This arrangement TRO - © Copyright 2019 Essex Music, Inc., Words and Music, Inc., New York, NY,
Don Swan Publications, Miami, FL and Gilbert Keyes Music, Hollywood, CA
International Copyright Secured
All Rights Reserved Including Public Performance For Profit
Used by Permission

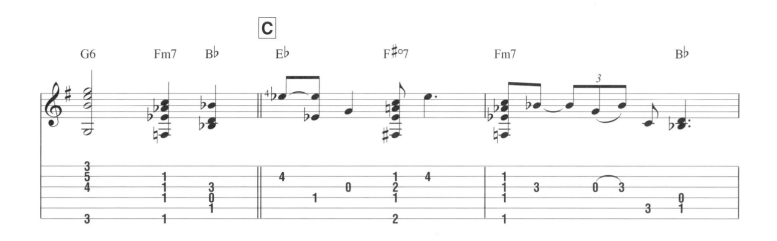

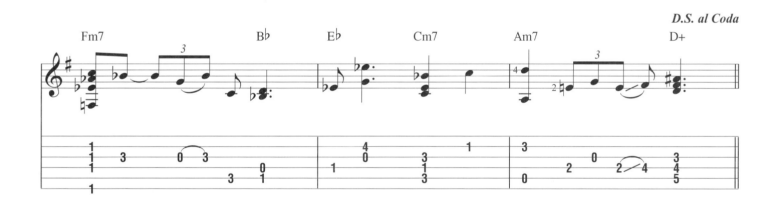

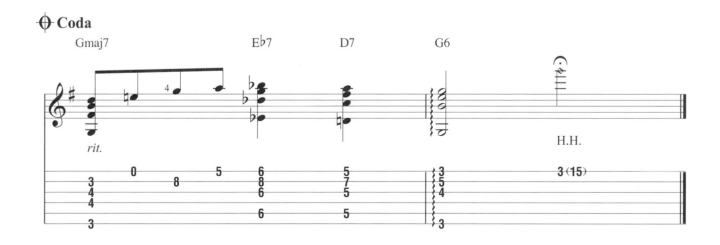

Embraceable You

from CRAZY FOR YOU

Music and Lyrics by George Gershwin and Ira Gershwin

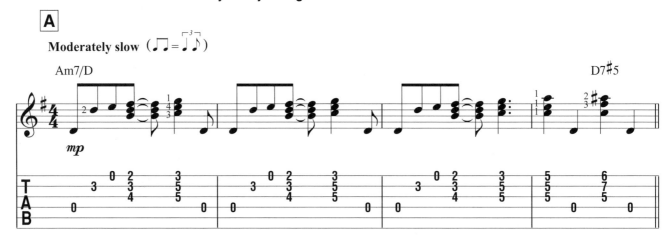

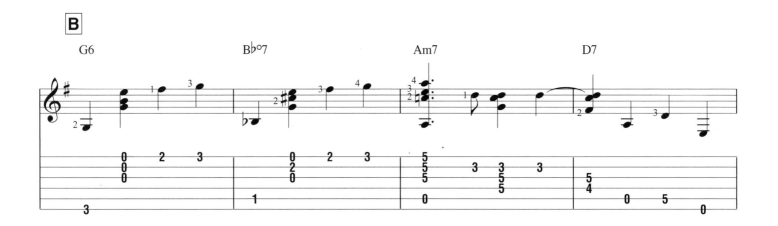

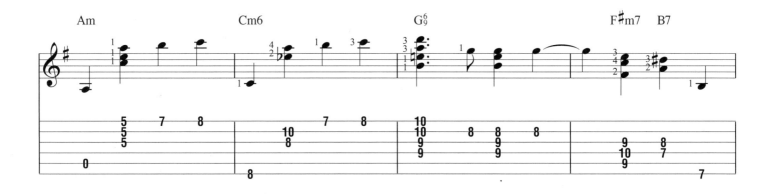

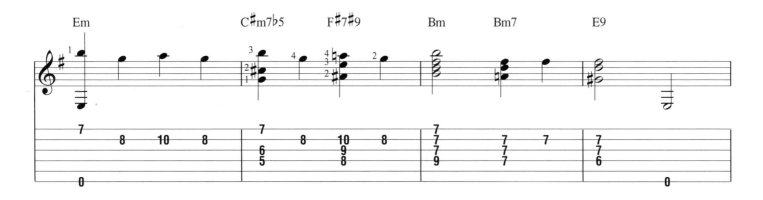

© 1930 (Renewed) WB MUSIC CORP.
This arrangement © 2019 WB MUSIC CORP.
All Rights Reserved   Used by Permission

*Optional: T = Thumb on 6th string

Gabriel's Oboe

from the Motion Picture THE MISSION

Music by Ennio Morricone

Drop D tuning:
(low to high) D-A-D-G-B-E

Moderately slow

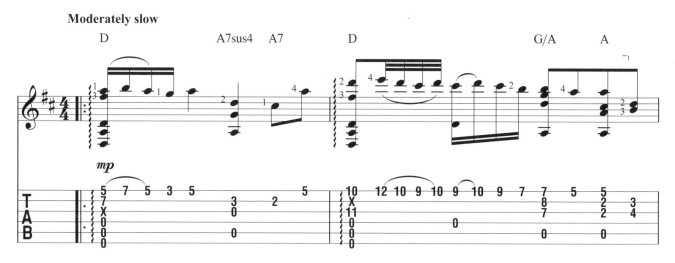

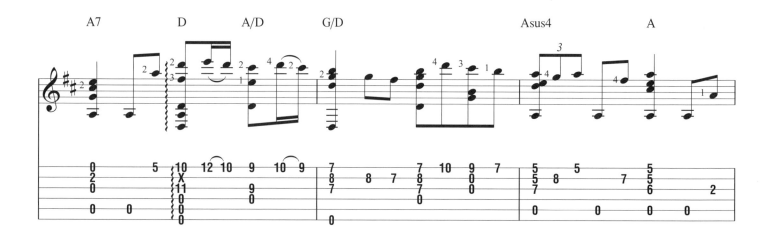

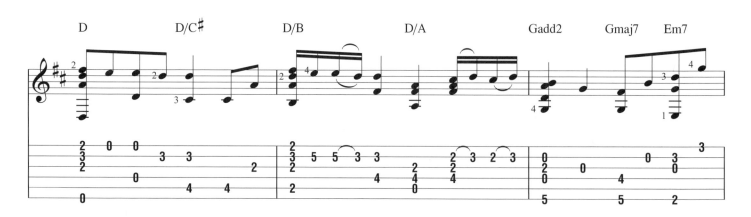

Copyright © 1986 BMG VM Music Ltd.
This arrangement Copyright © 2019 BMG VM Music Ltd.
All Rights Administered by BMG Rights Management (US) LLC
All Rights Reserved   Used by Permission

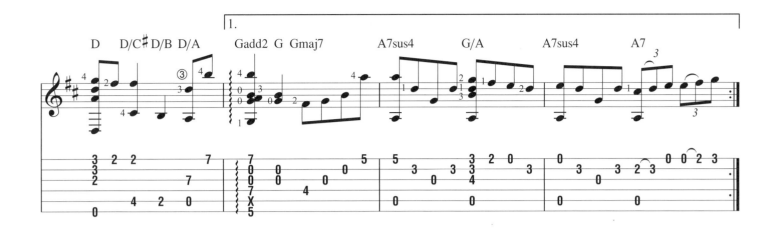

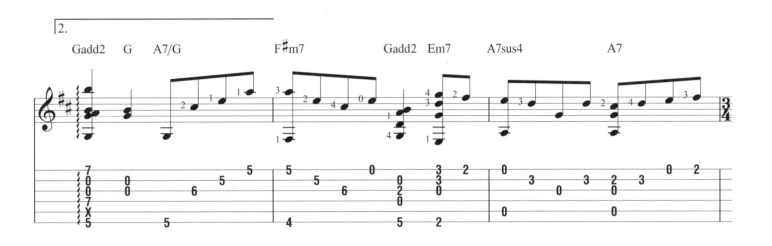

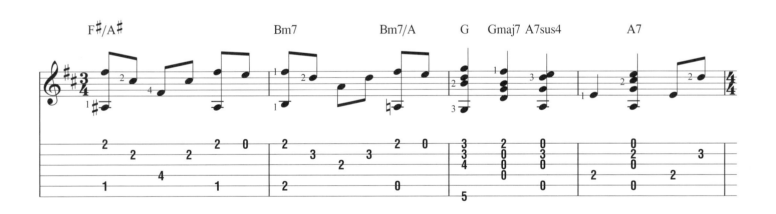

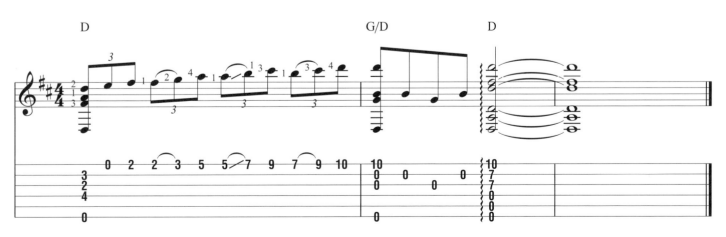

The Godfather
(Love Theme)
from the Paramount Picture THE GODFATHER
By Nino Rota

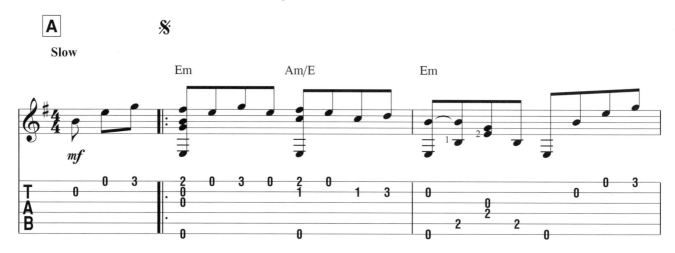

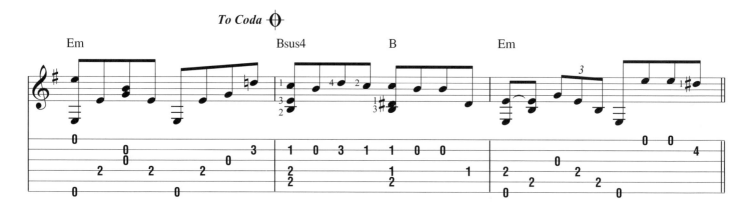

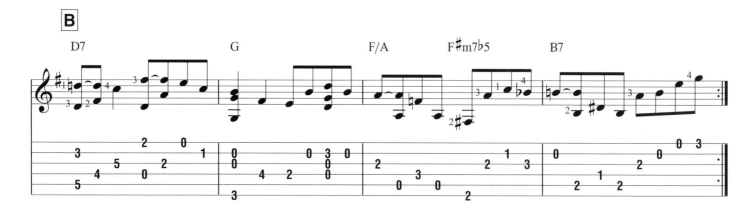

Copyright © 1972 Sony/ATV Music Publishing LLC
Copyright Renewed
This arrangement Copyright © 2019 Sony/ATV Music Publishing LLC
All Rights Administered by Sony/ATV Music Publishing LLC, 424 Church Street, Suite 1200, Nashville, TN 37219
International Copyright Secured   All Rights Reserved

D.S. al Coda

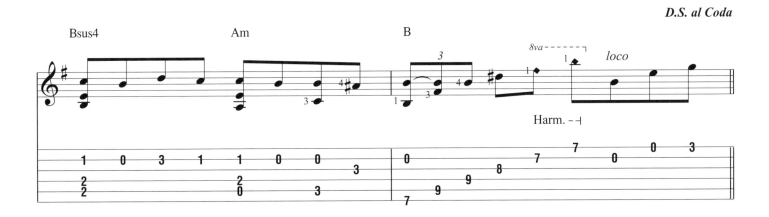

Hallelujah

Words and Music by Leonard Cohen

Copyright © 1985 Sony/ATV Music Publishing LLC
This arrangement Copyright © 2019 Sony/ATV Music Publishing LLC
All Rights Administered by Sony/ATV Music Publishing LLC, 424 Church Street, Suite 1200, Nashville, TN 37219
International Copyright Secured   All Rights Reserved

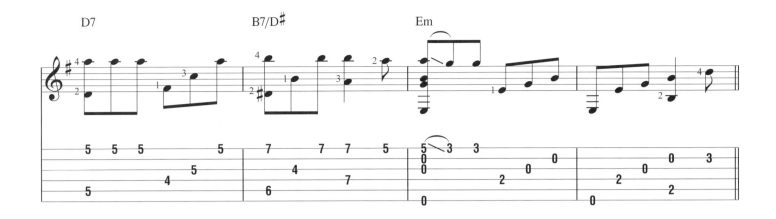

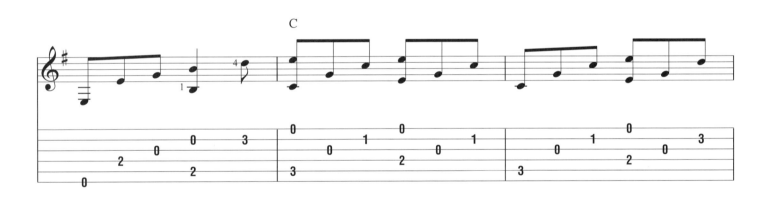

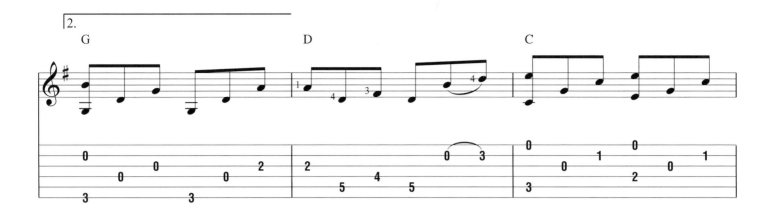

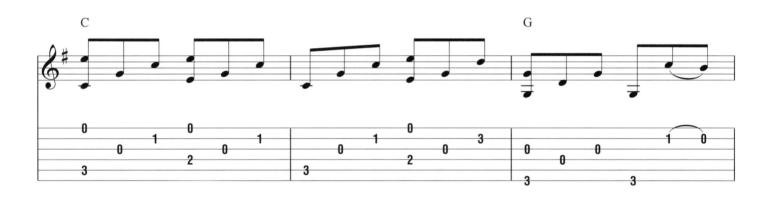

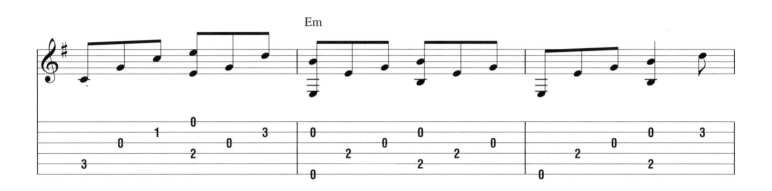

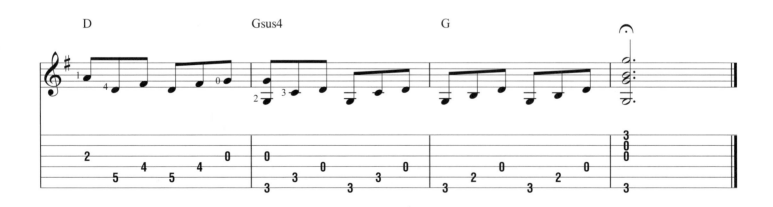

He's a Pirate

from PIRATES OF THE CARIBBEAN: THE CURSE OF THE BLACK PEARL

Written by Hans Zimmer, Klaus Badelt and Geoff Zanelli

Drop D tuning:
(low to high) D-A-D-G-B-E

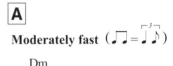

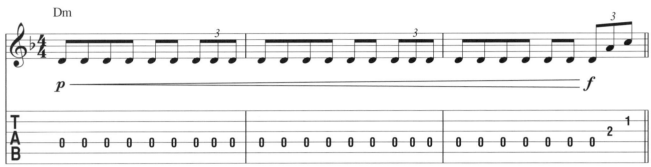

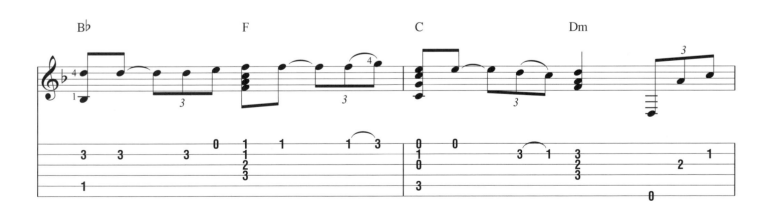

© 2003 Walt Disney Music Company
All Rights Reserved. Used by Permission.

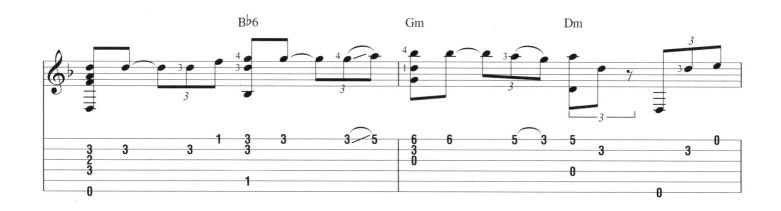

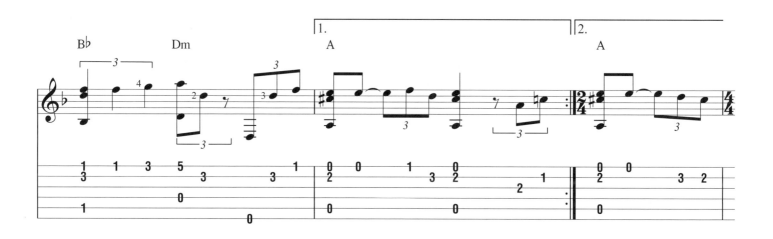

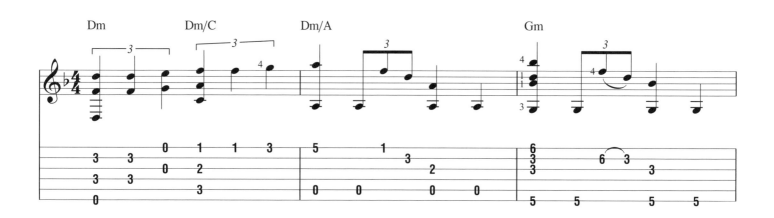

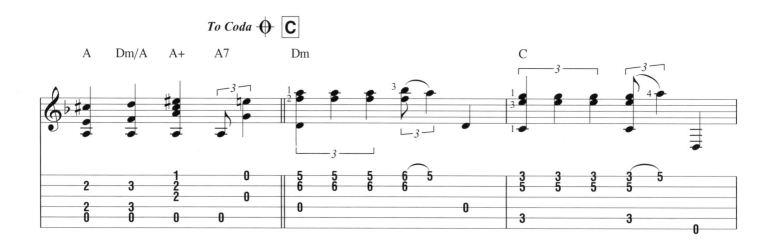

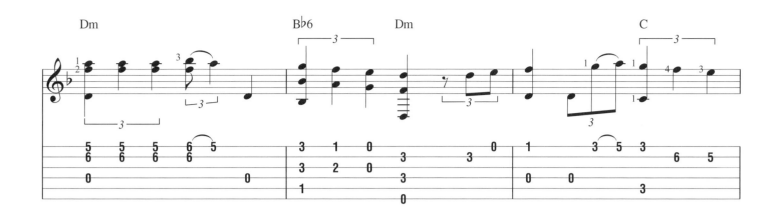

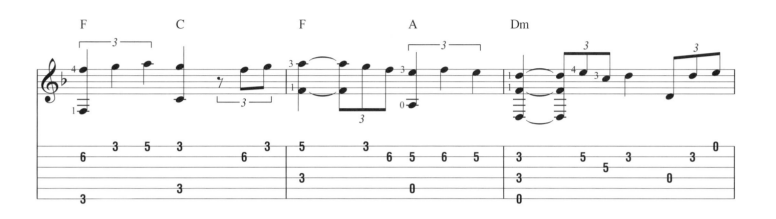

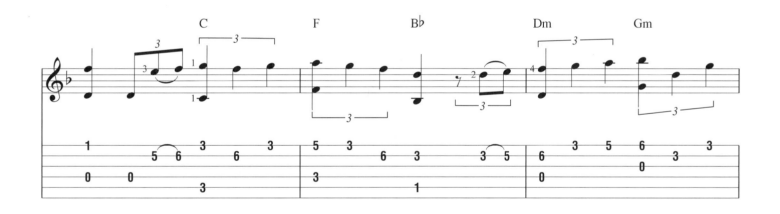

D.S. al Coda
(take 2nd ending)

⊕ Coda

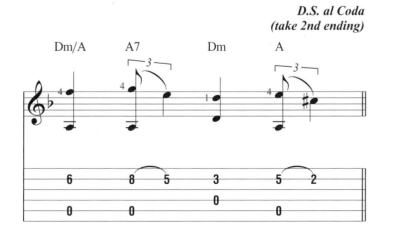

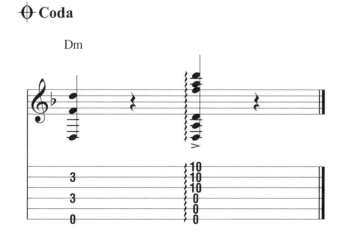

Hello

Words and Music by Adele Adkins and Greg Kurstin

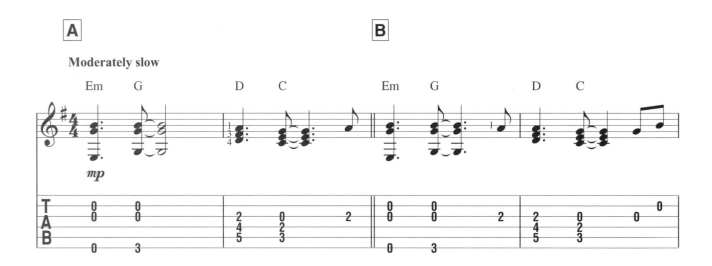

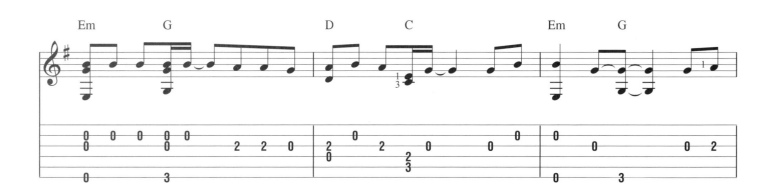

Copyright © 2015 MELTED STONE PUBLISHING LTD., EMI APRIL MUSIC INC. and KURSTIN MUSIC
This arrangement Copyright © 2019 MELTED STONE PUBLISHING LTD., EMI APRIL MUSIC INC. and KURSTIN MUSIC
All Rights for MELTED STONE PUBLISHING LTD. in the U.S. and Canada Administered by UNIVERSAL - SONGS OF POLYGRAM INTERNATIONAL, INC.
All Rights for EMI APRIL MUSIC INC. and KURSTIN MUSIC Administered by
SONY/ATV MUSIC PUBLISHING LLC, 424 Church Street, Suite 1200, Nashville, TN 37219
All Rights Reserved   Used by Permission

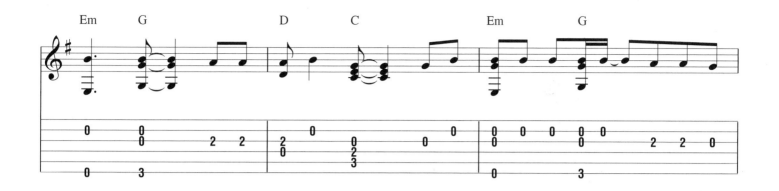

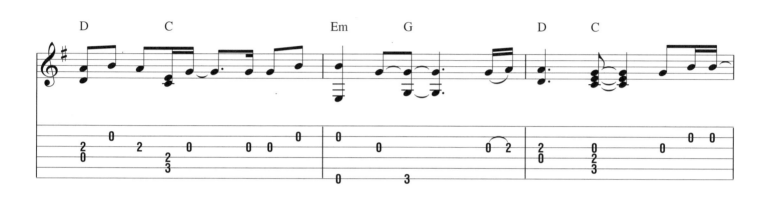

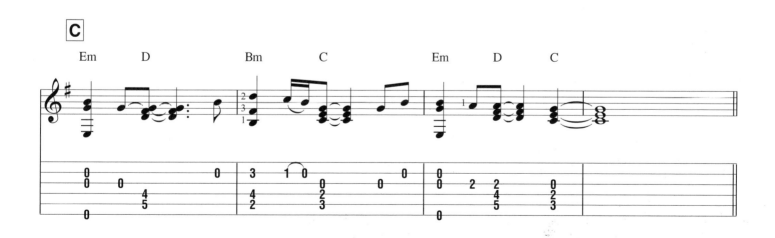

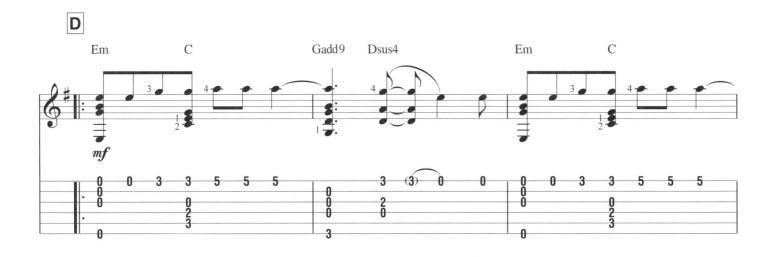

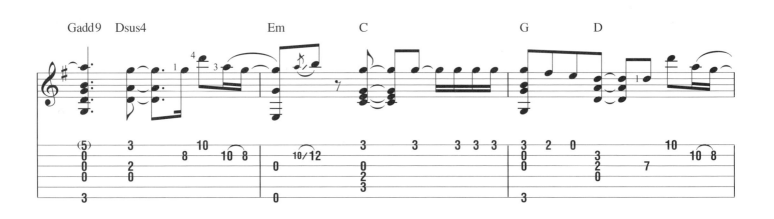

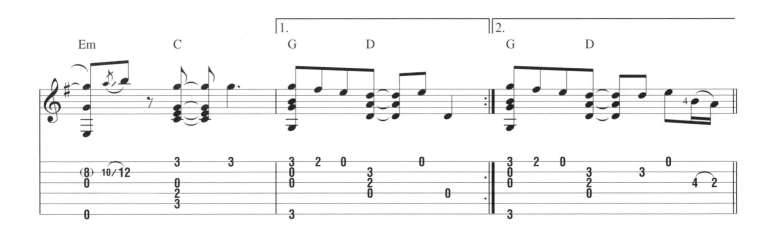

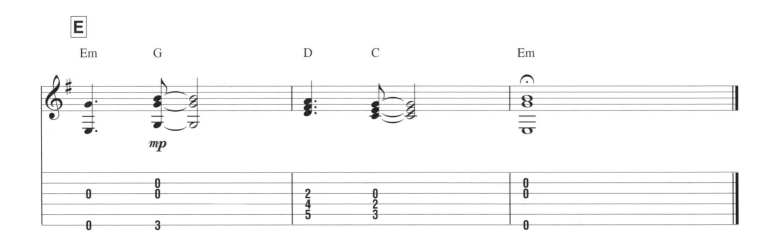

How Deep Is Your Love

from the Motion Picture SATURDAY NIGHT FEVER

Words and Music by Barry Gibb, Robin Gibb and Maurice Gibb

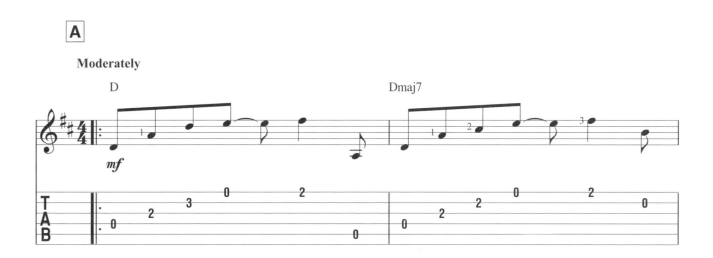

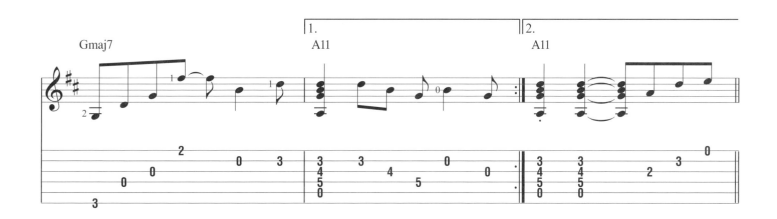

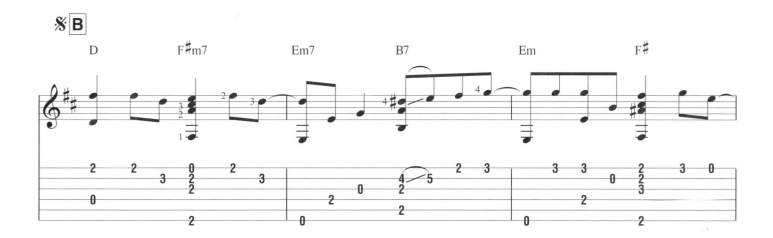

Copyright © 1979 CROMPTON SONGS, REDBREAST PUBLISHING LTD. and UNIVERSAL MUSIC PUBLISHING INTERNATIONAL MGB LTD.
This arrangement Copyright © 2019 CROMPTON SONGS, REDBREAST PUBLISHING LTD.
and UNIVERSAL MUSIC PUBLISHING INTERNATIONAL MGB LTD.
All Rights for CROMPTON SONGS Administered by SONGS OF UNIVERSAL, INC.
All Rights for REDBREAST PUBLISHING LTD. and UNIVERSAL MUSIC PUBLISHING INTERNATIONAL MGB LTD.
Administered by UNIVERSAL MUSIC - CAREERS
All Rights Reserved   Used by Permission

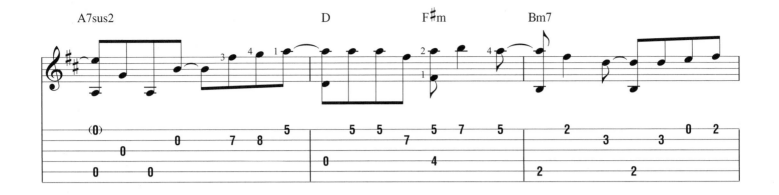

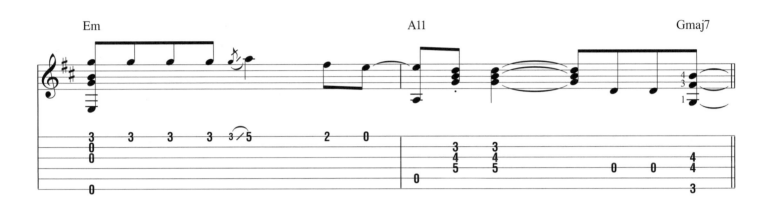

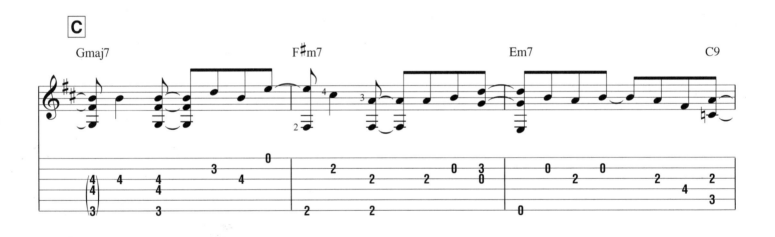

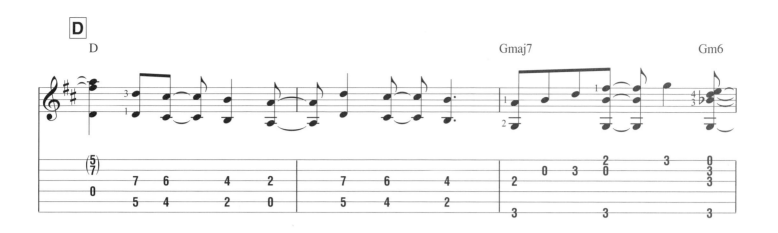

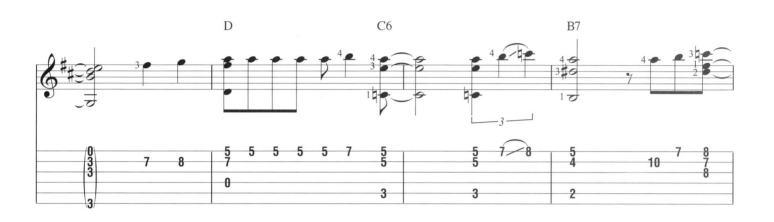

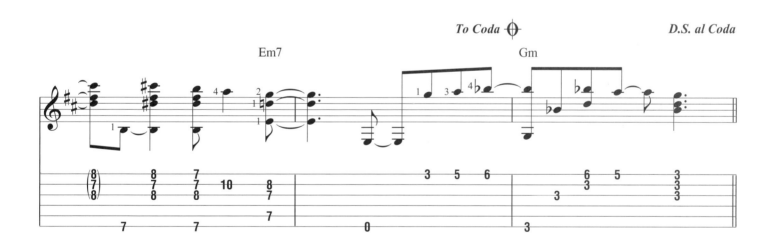

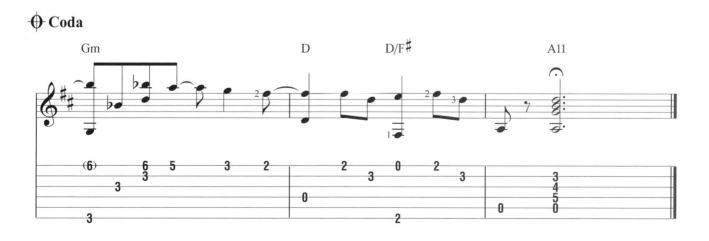

I Just Called to Say I Love You

from THE WOMAN IN RED

Words and Music by Stevie Wonder

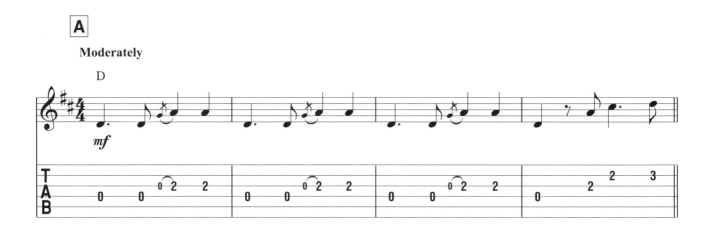

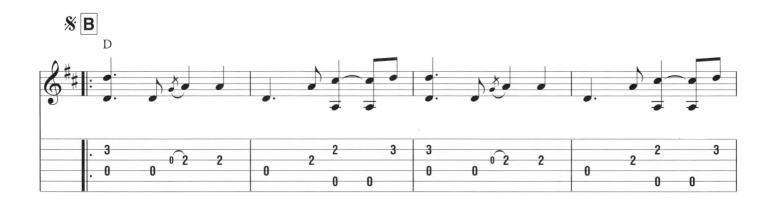

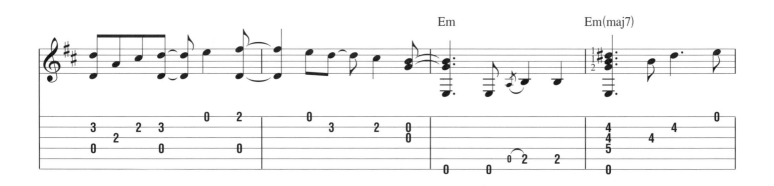

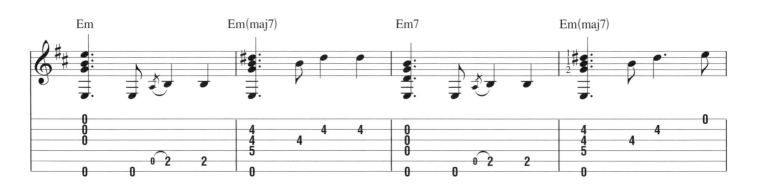

Copyright © 1984 Jobete Music Co., Inc. and Black Bull Music
This arrangement Copyright © 2019 Jobete Music Co., Inc. and Black Bull Music
All Rights Administered by Sony/ATV Music Publishing LLC, 424 Church Street, Suite 1200, Nashville, TN 37219
International Copyright Secured   All Rights Reserved

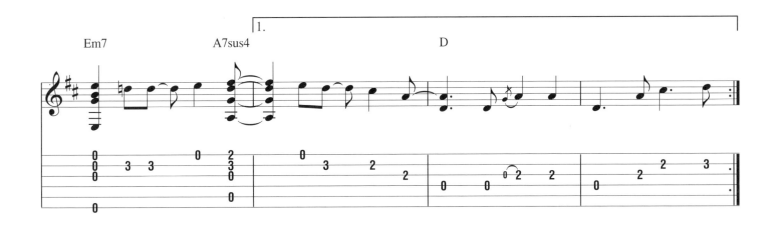

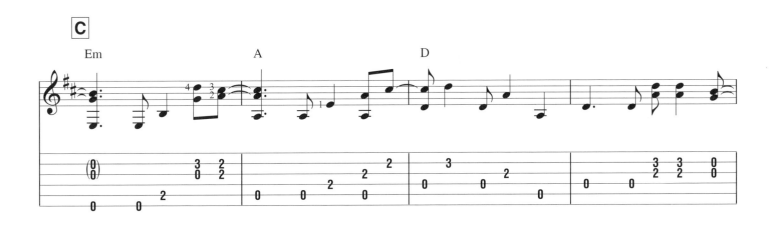

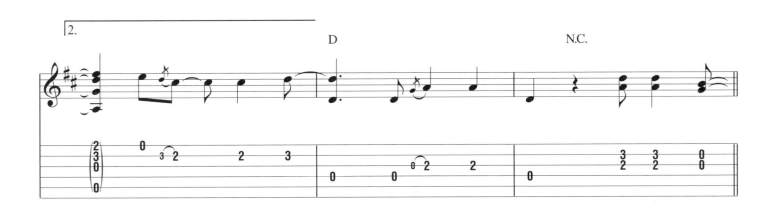

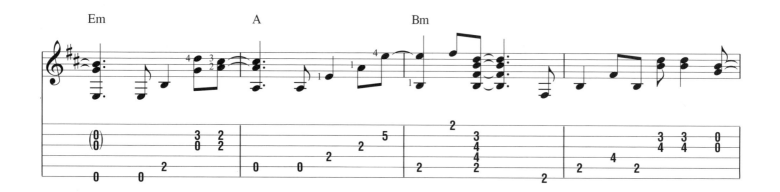

To Coda ⊕

D.S. al Coda
(take repeat)

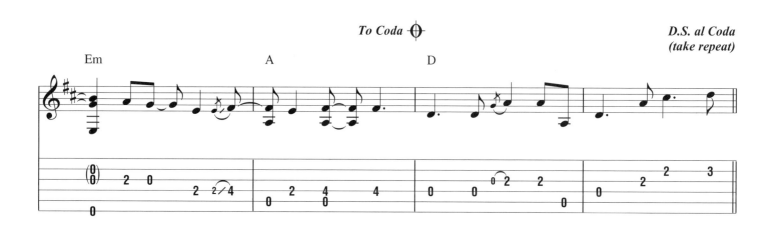

⊕ **Coda**

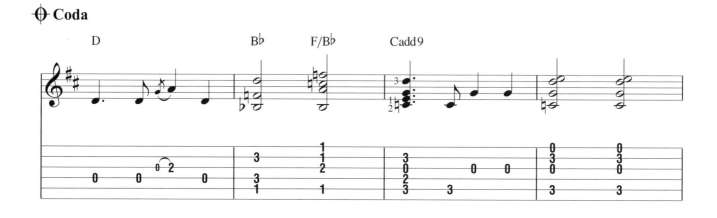

My Favorite Things

from THE SOUND OF MUSIC

Lyrics by Oscar Hammerstein II
Music by Richard Rodgers

A

Moderately

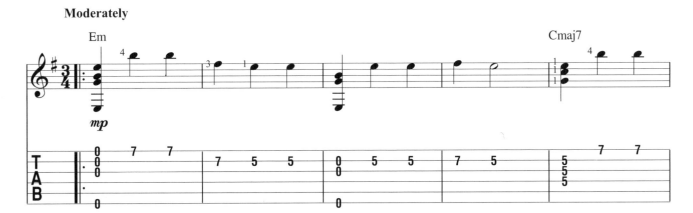

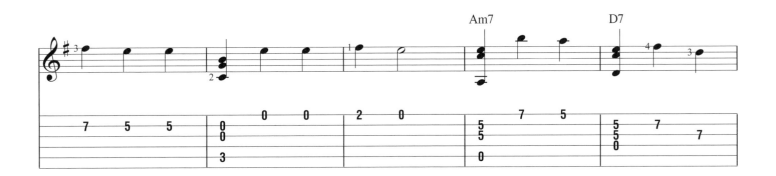

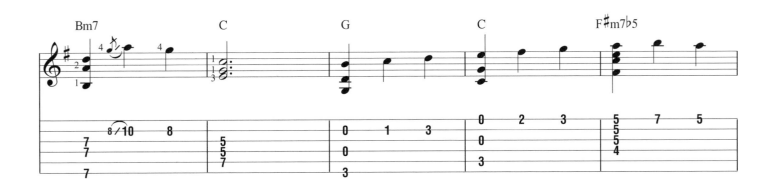

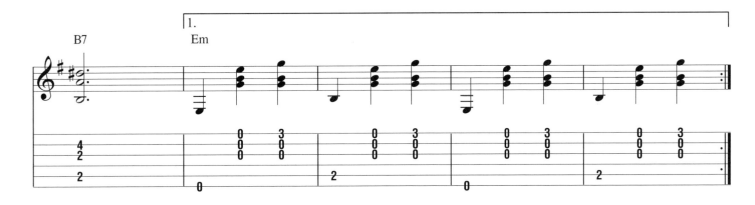

Copyright © 1959 by Richard Rodgers and Oscar Hammerstein II
Copyright Renewed
This arrangement Copyright © 2019 by Williamson Music
Williamson Music, a Division of Rodgers & Hammerstein: an Imagem Company, owner of publication and allied rights throughout the world
International Copyright Secured   All Rights Reserved

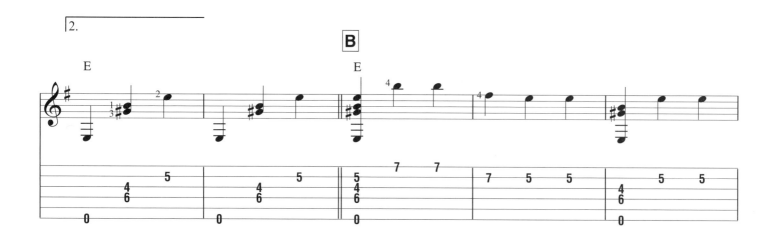

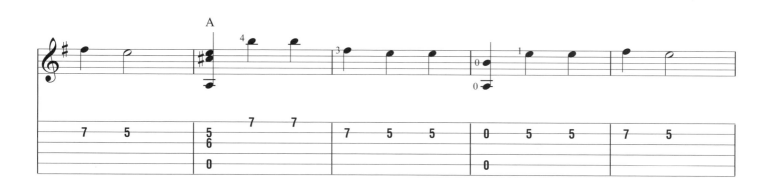

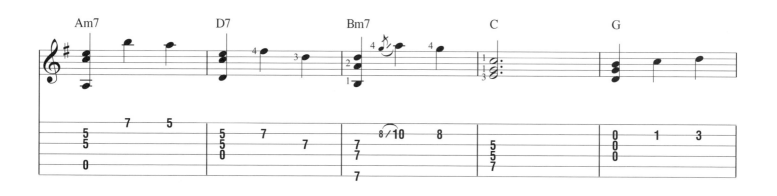

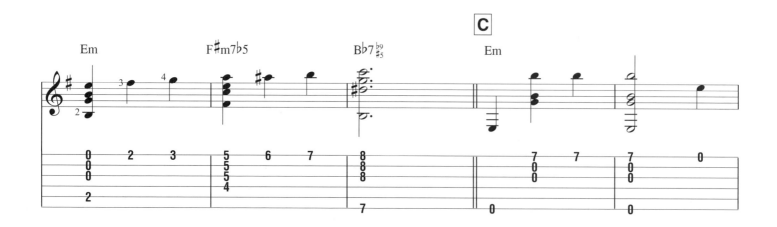

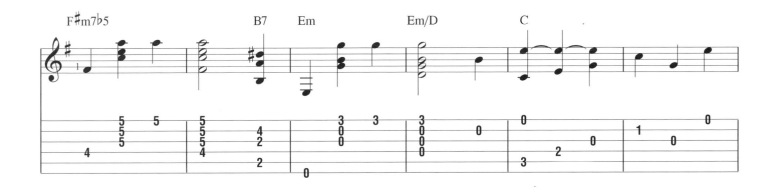

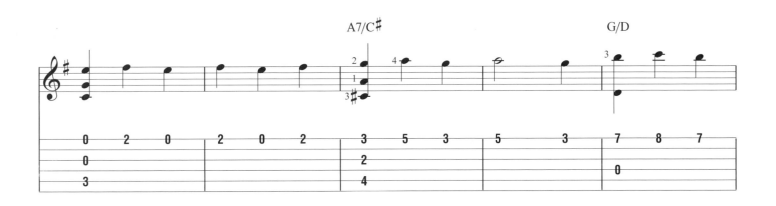

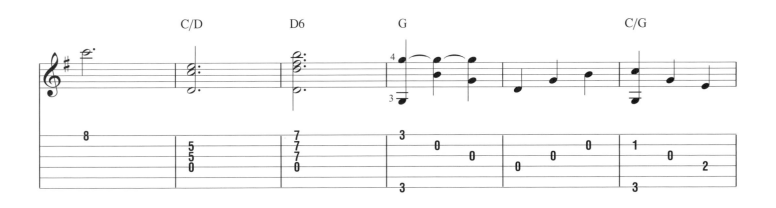

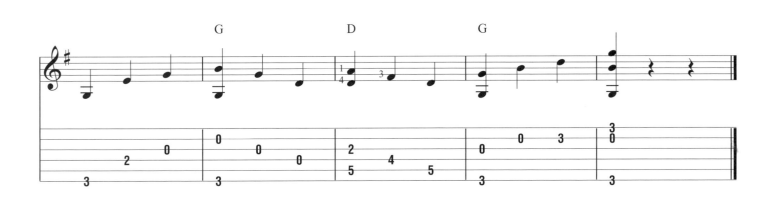

In My Life

Words and Music by John Lennon and Paul McCartney

Copyright © 1965 Sony/ATV Music Publishing LLC
Copyright Renewed
This arrangement Copyright © 2019 Sony/ATV Music Publishing LLC
All Rights Administered by Sony/ATV Music Publishing LLC, 424 Church Street, Suite 1200, Nashville, TN 37219
International Copyright Secured   All Rights Reserved

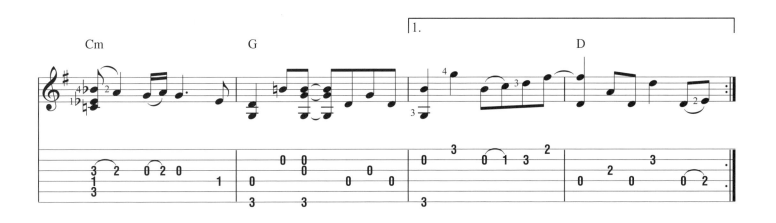

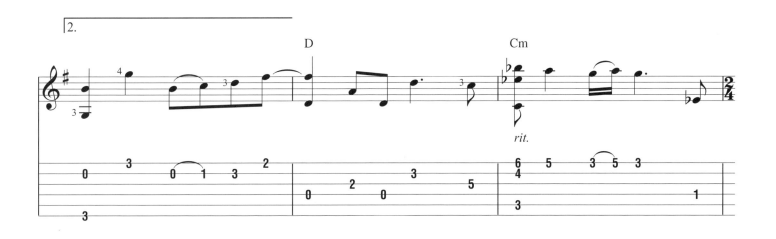

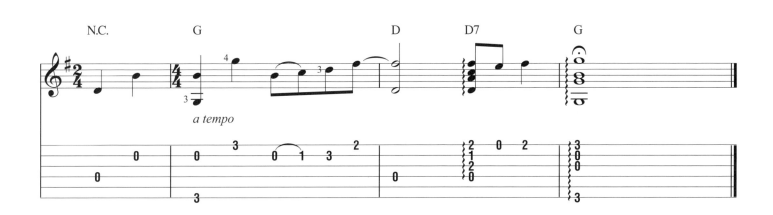

Killing Me Softly with His Song

Words by Norman Gimbel
Music by Charles Fox

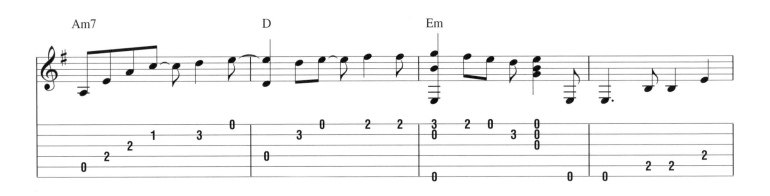

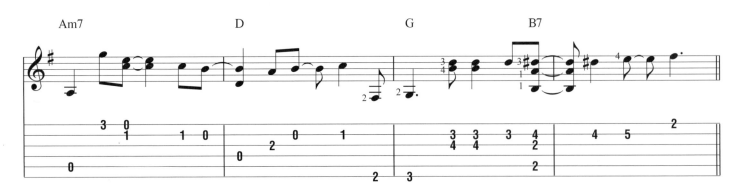

© 1972 (Renewed) RODALI MUSIC and WORDS WEST LLC (P.O. Box 15187, Beverly Hills, CA 90209 USA)
This arrangement © 2019 RODALI MUSIC and WORDS WEST LLC (P.O. Box 15187, Beverly Hills, CA 90209 USA)
All Rights for RODALI MUSIC Administered by WARNER-TAMERLANE PUBLISHING CORP.
All Rights Reserved   Used by Permission

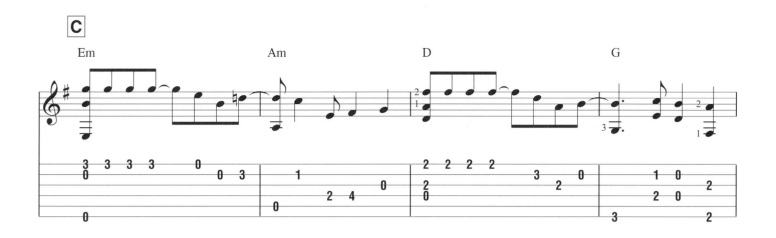

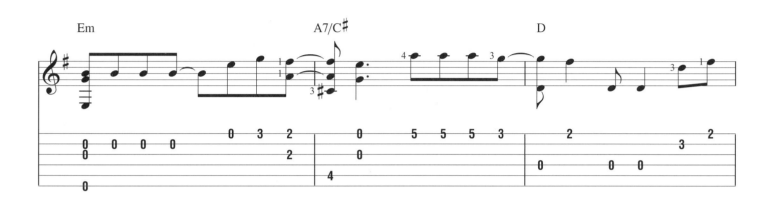

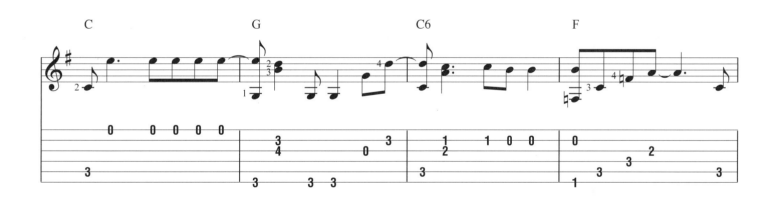

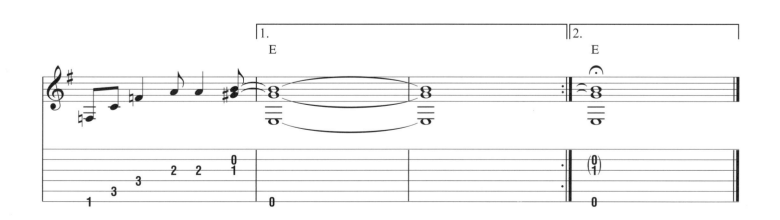

La Vie en Rose
(Take Me to Your Heart Again)

Original French Lyrics by Edith Piaf
Music by Louiguy
English Lyrics by Mack David

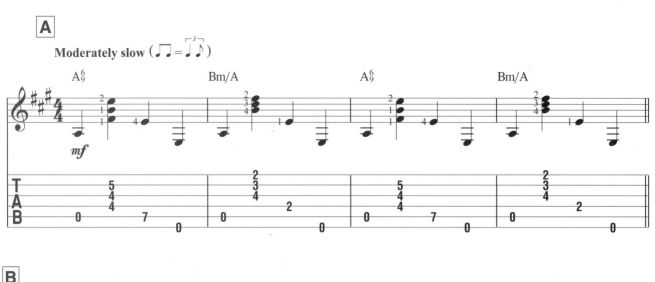

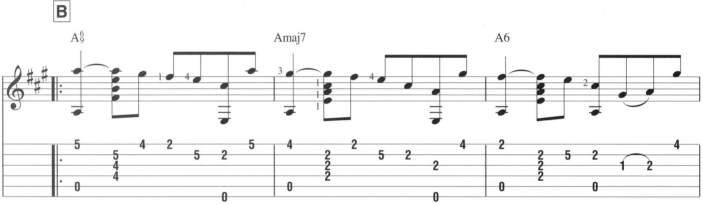

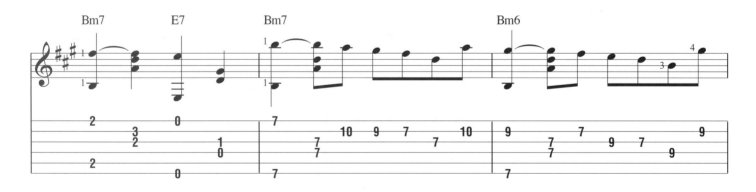

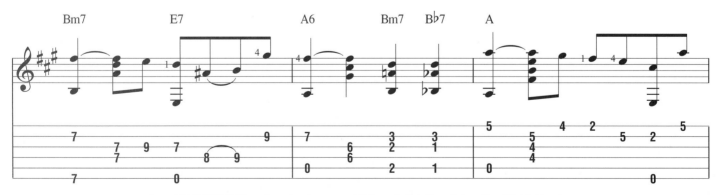

Copyright © 1950 Editions Beuscher Arpege and Univeral - PolyGram International Publishing, Inc.
Copyright Renewed
This arrangement Copyright © 2019 Editions Beuscher Arpege and Universal - PolyGram International Publishing, Inc.
All Rights on behalf of Editions Beuscher Arpege Administered by
Sony/ATV Music Publishing LLC, 424 Church Street, Suite 1200, Nashville, TN 37219
International Copyright Secured   All Rights Reserved

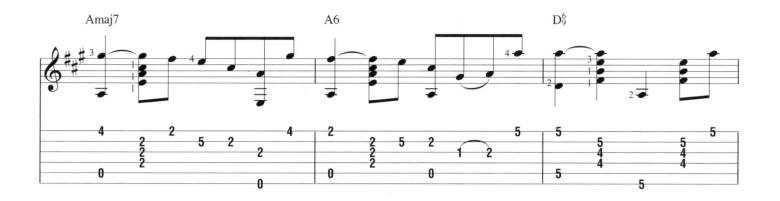

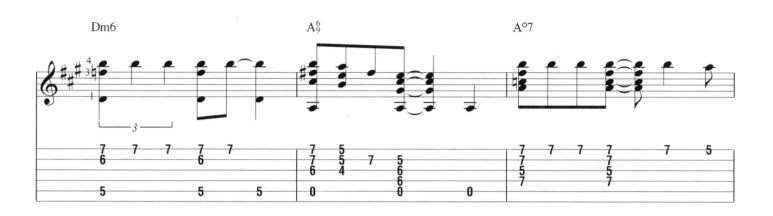

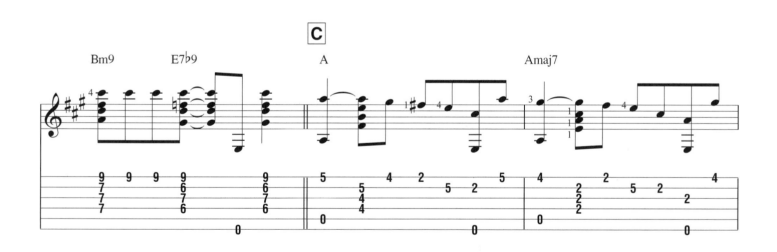

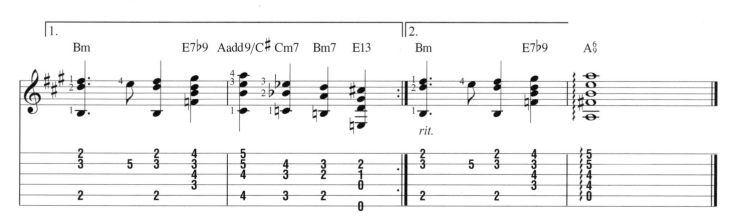

Little Wing

Words and Music by Jimi Hendrix

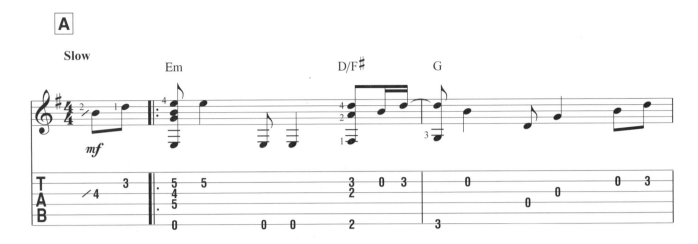

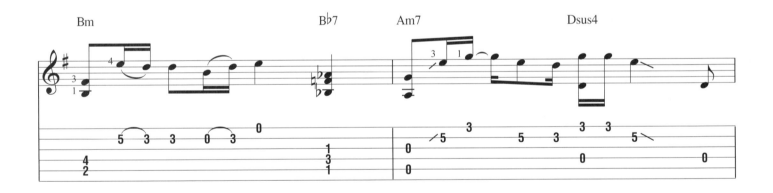

Copyright © 1968 by EXPERIENCE HENDRIX, L.L.C.
Copyright Renewed 1996
This arrangement Copyright © 2019 by EXPERIENCE HENDRIX, L.L.C.
All Rights Controlled and Administered by EXPERIENCE HENDRIX, L.L.C.
All Rights Reserved

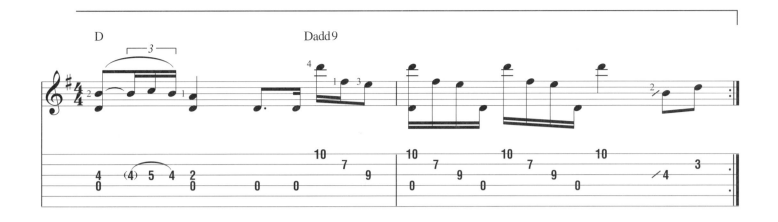

More
(Ti Guarderò Nel Cuore)
from the film MONDO CANE
Music by Nino Oliviero and Riz Ortolani
Italian Lyrics by Marcello Ciorciolini
English Lyrics by Norman Newell

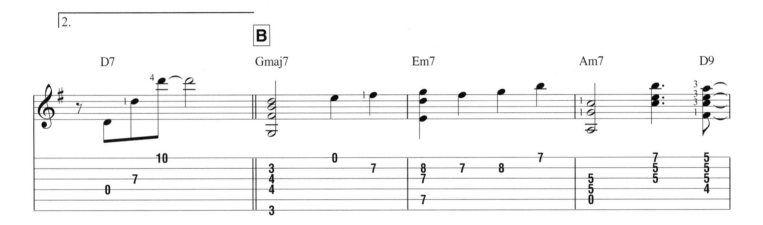

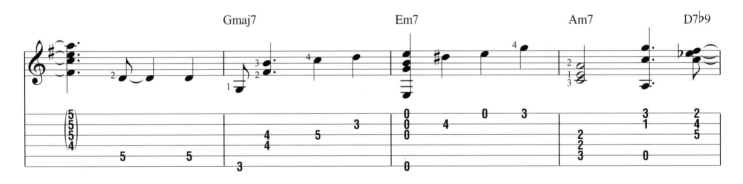

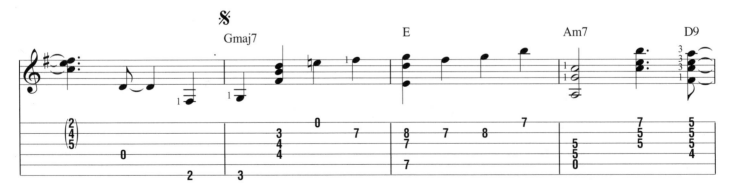

Copyright © 1962 Creazioni Artistiche Musicali C.A.M. S.r.l. and CTC Creative Team Company
Copyright Renewed
This arrangement Copyright © 2019 Creazioni Artistiche Musicali C.A.M. S.r.l. and CTC Creative Team Company
International Copyright Secured   All Rights Reserved

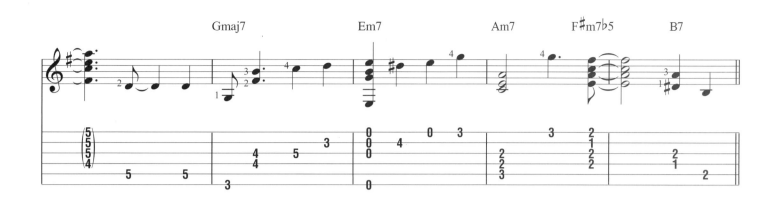

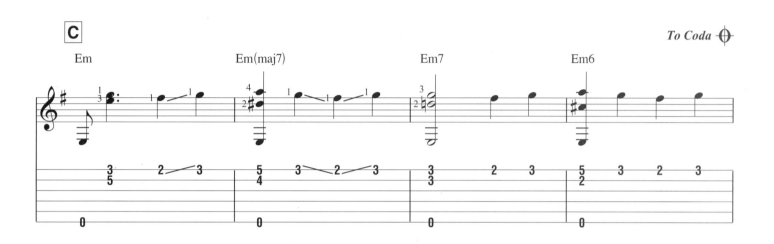

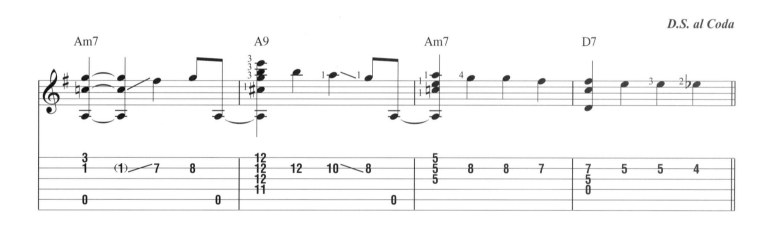

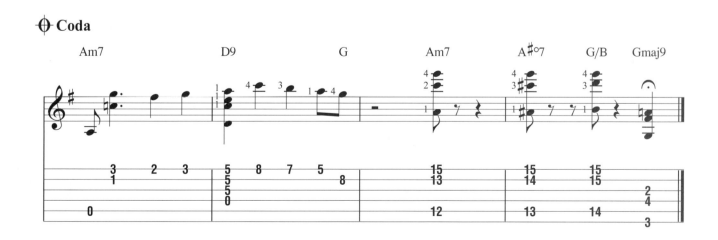

Oblivion

By Astor Piazzolla

 A

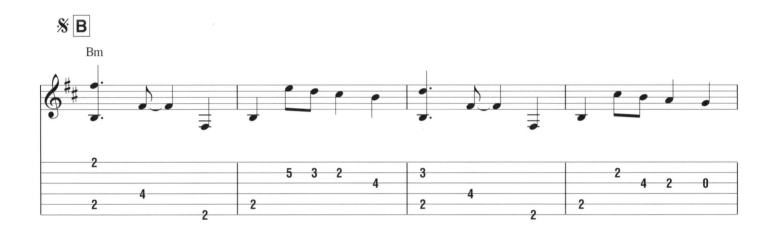

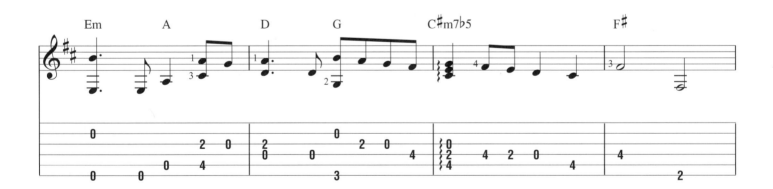

© 1984 by A. PAGANI S.r.l. Edizioni Musicali
This arrangement © 2019 by A. PAGANI S.r.l. Edizioni Musicali
Rights for USA Controlled by Downtown DLJ Songs o/b/o Edward Kassner Music Co. Ltd.
All Rights Reserved   Used by Permission

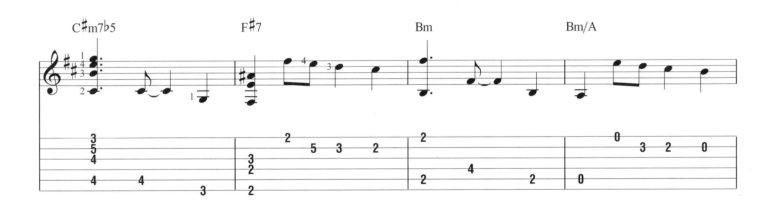

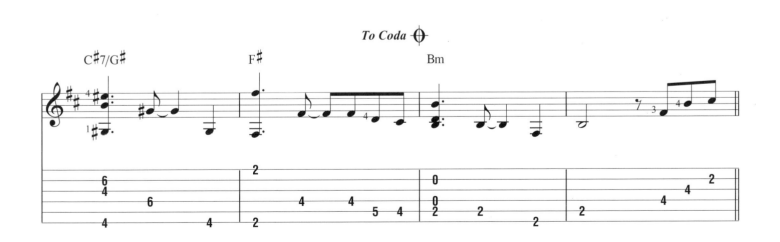

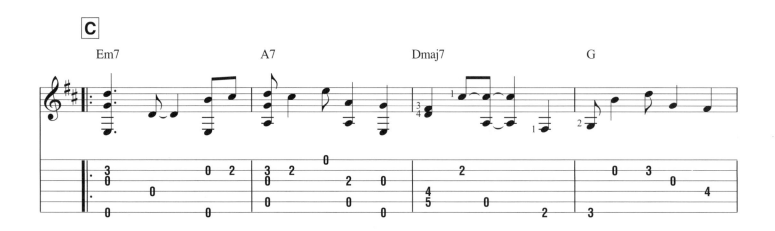

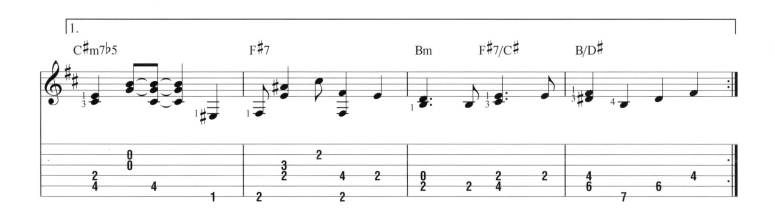

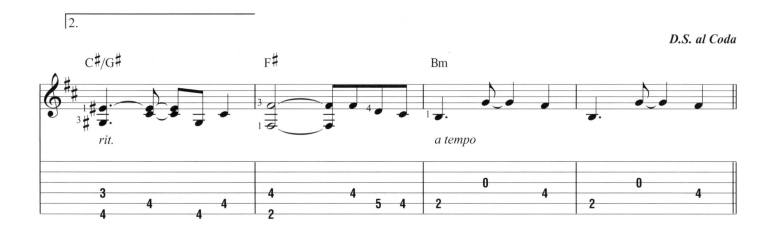

 Coda

One of Us

Words and Music by Eric Bazilian

© 1995 HUMAN BOY MUSIC
This arrangement © 2019 HUMAN BOY MUSIC
All Rights Administered by WB MUSIC CORP.
All Rights Reserved   Used by Permission

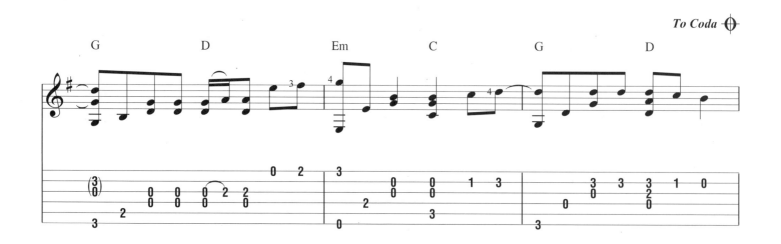

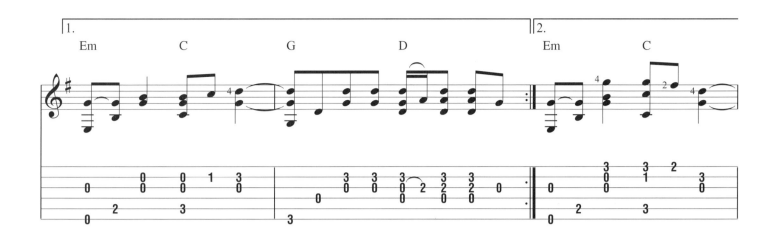

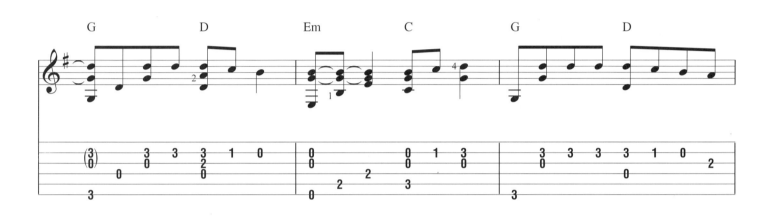

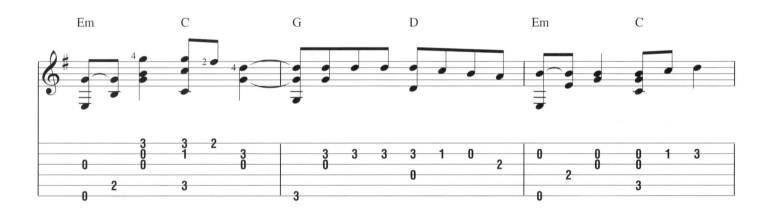

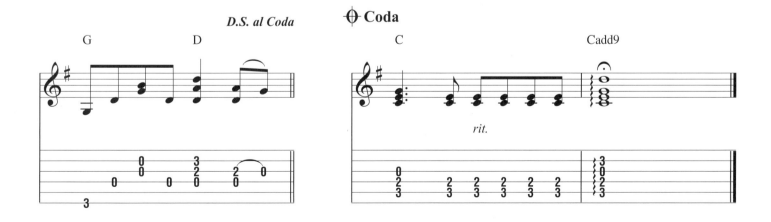

Over the Rainbow

from THE WIZARD OF OZ

Music by Harold Arlen
Lyric by E.Y. "Yip" Harburg

© 1938 (Renewed) METRO-GOLDWYN-MAYER INC.
© 1939 (Renewed) EMI FEIST CATALOG INC.
This arrangement © 2019 METRO-GOLDWYN-MAYER INC. and EMI FEIST CATALOG INC.
All Rights Administered by EMI FEIST CATALOG INC. (Publishing) and ALFRED MUSIC (Print)
All Rights Reserved   Used by Permission

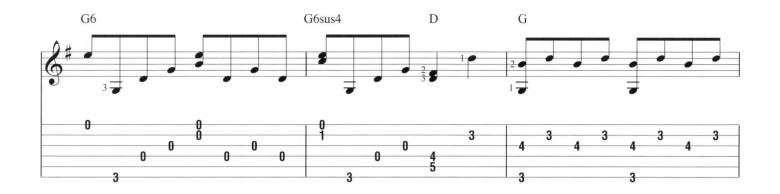

D.C. al Coda

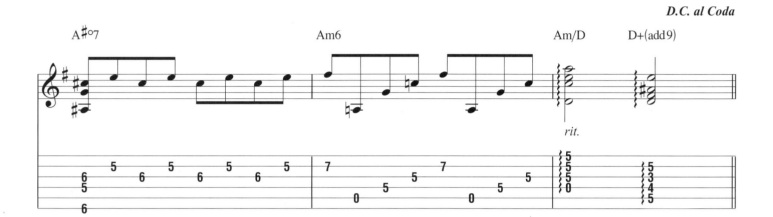

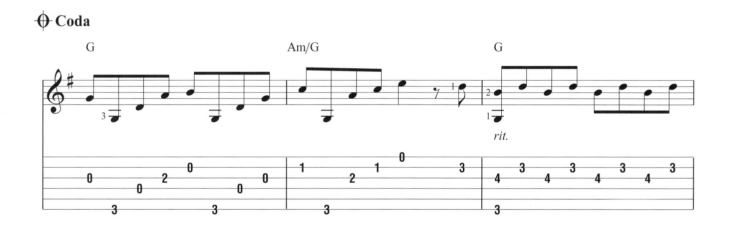

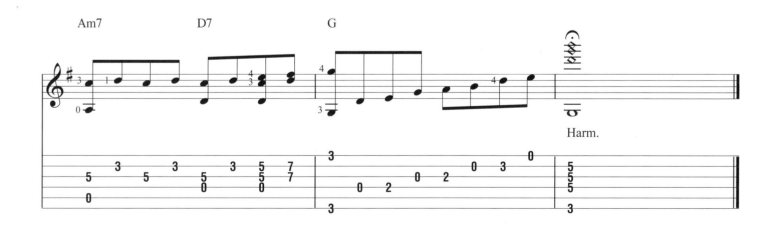

People Get Ready

Words and Music by Curtis Mayfield

Copyright © 1964, 1965 Mijac Music and Warner-Tamerlane Publishing Corp.
Copyright Renewed
This arrangement Copyright © 2019 Mijac Music and Warner-Tamerlane Publishing Corp.
All Rights on behalf of Mijac Music Administered by Sony/ATV Music Publishing LLC, 424 Church Street, Suite 1200, Nashville, TN 37219
International Copyright Secured   All Rights Reserved

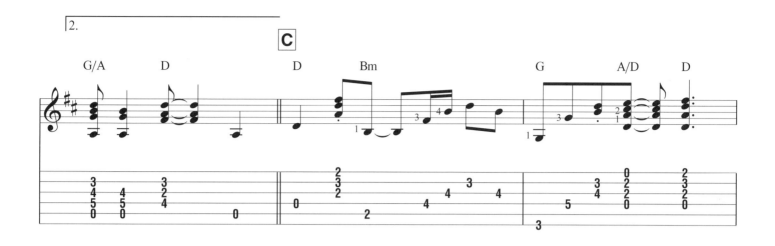

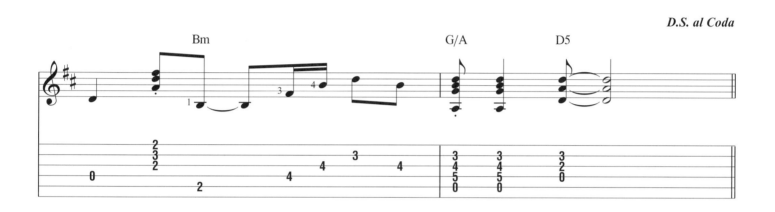

D.S. al Coda

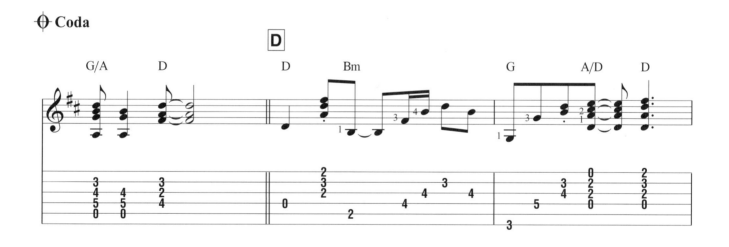

⊕ Coda

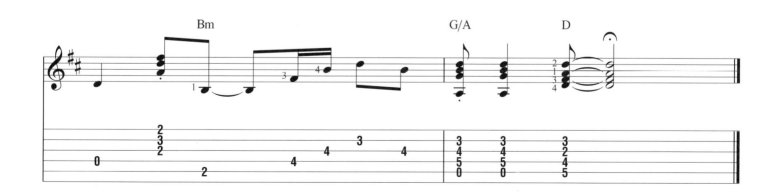

Perfect

Words and Music by Ed Sheeran

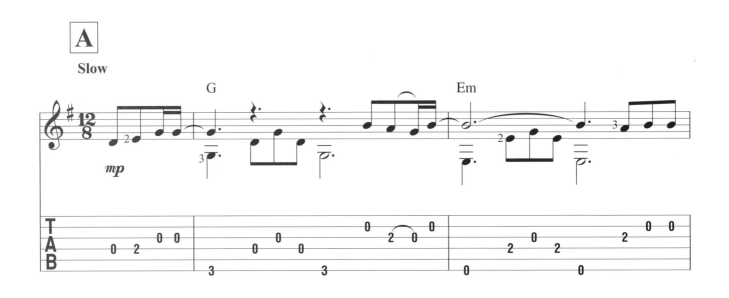

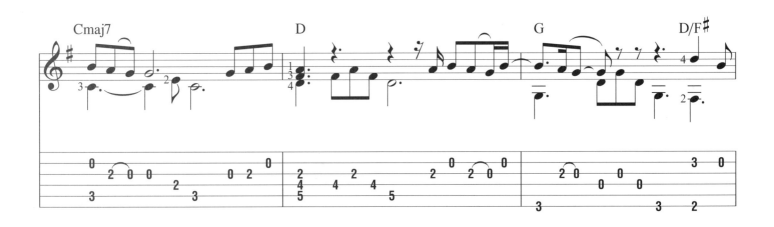

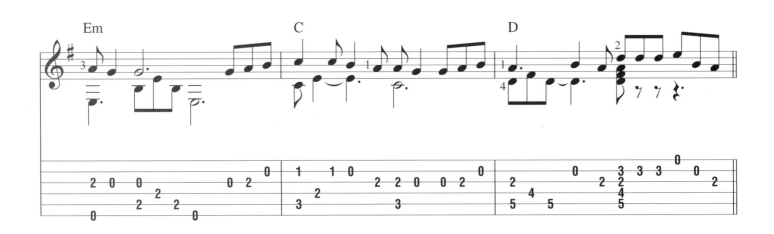

Copyright © 2017 Sony/ATV Music Publishing (UK) Limited
This arrangement Copyright © 2020 Sony/ATV Music Publishing (UK) Limited
All Rights Administered by Sony/ATV Music Publishing (US) LLC, 424 Church Street, Suite 1200, Nashville, TN 37219
International Copyright Secured   All Rights Reserved

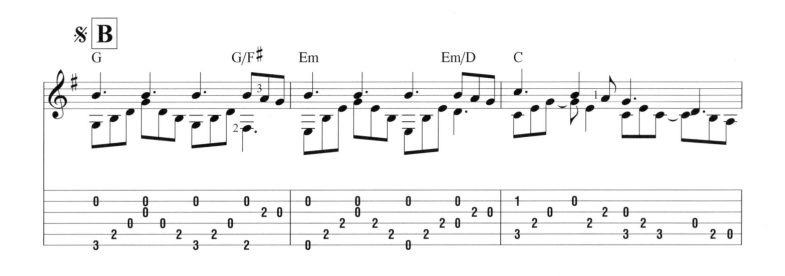

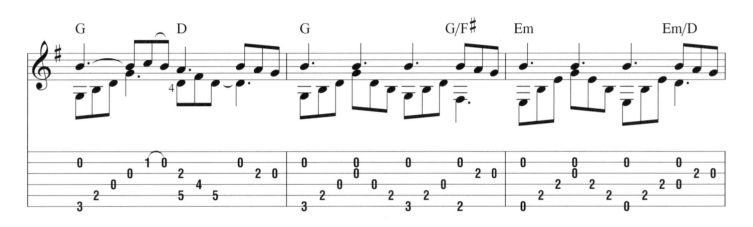

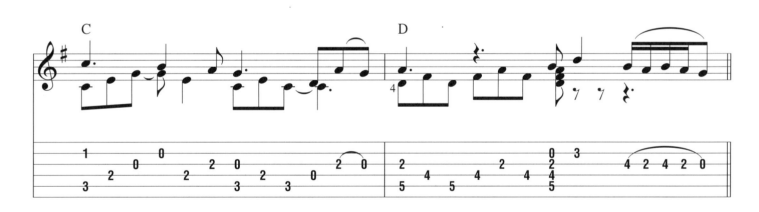

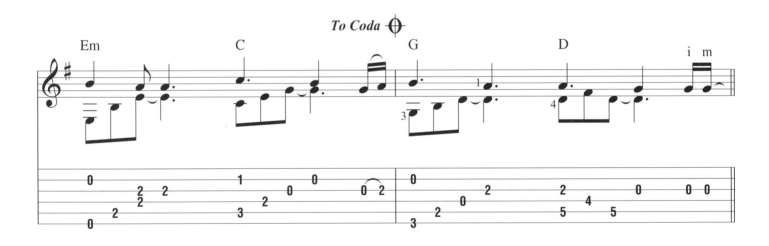

D

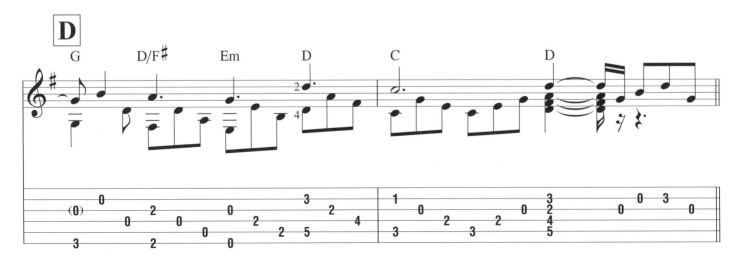

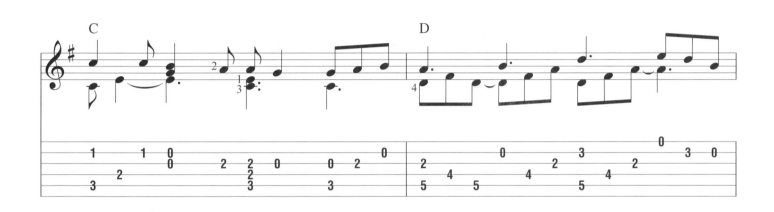

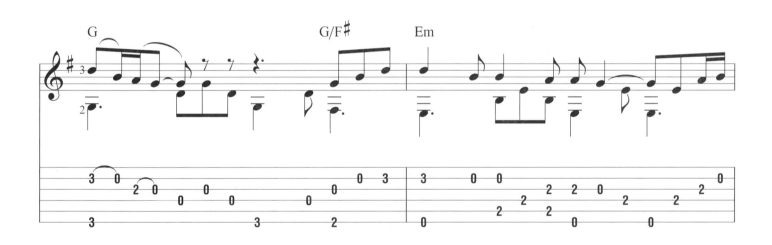

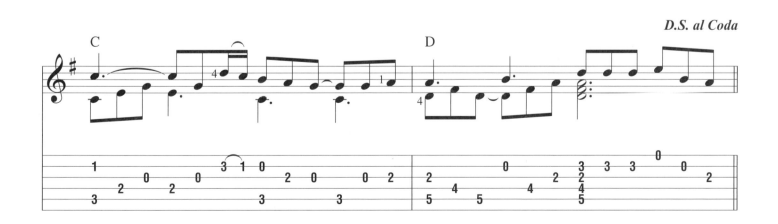

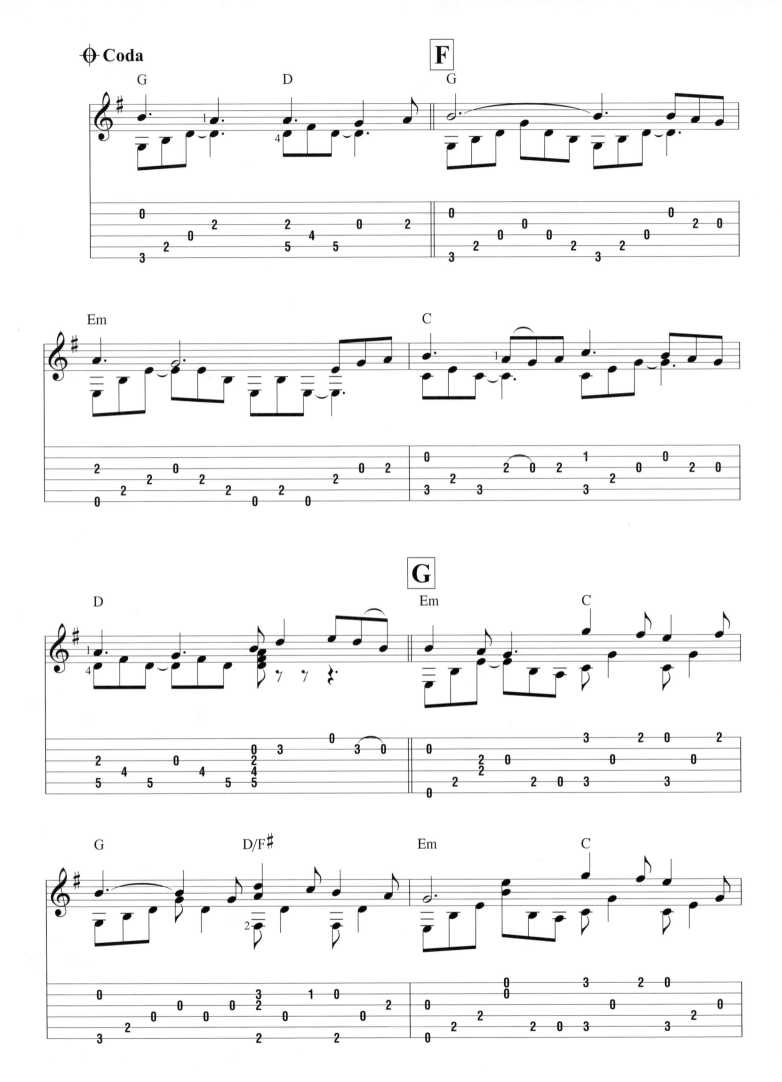

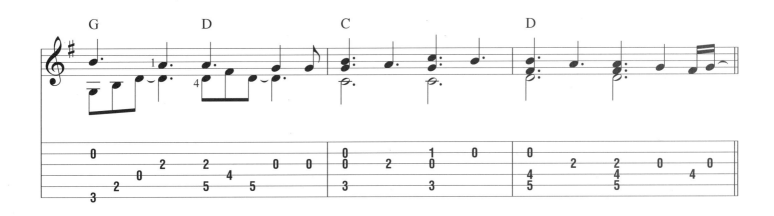

H

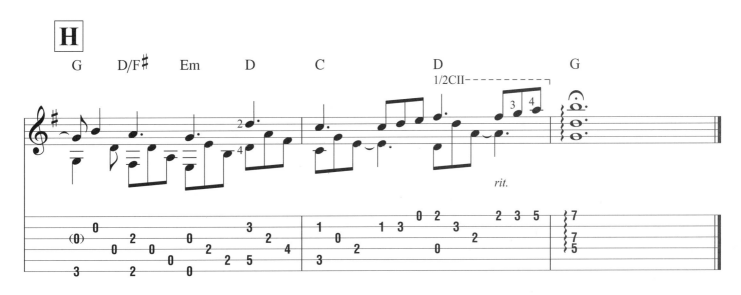

The Pink Panther

from THE PINK PANTHER

By Henry Mancini

Copyright © 1963 Northridge Music Company and EMI U Catalog Inc.
Copyright Renewed
This arrangement Copyright © 2019 Northridge Music Company and EMI U Catalog Inc.
All Rights on behalf of Northridge Music Company Administered by Spirit Two Music
Exclusive Print Rights for EMI U Catalog Inc. Controlled and Administered by Alfred Music
All Rights Reserved   Used by Permission

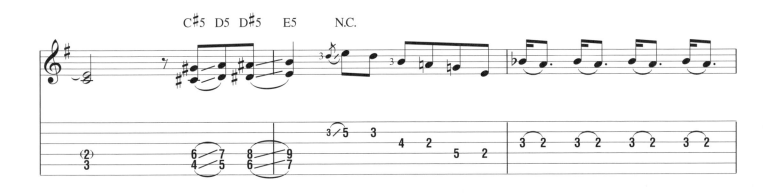

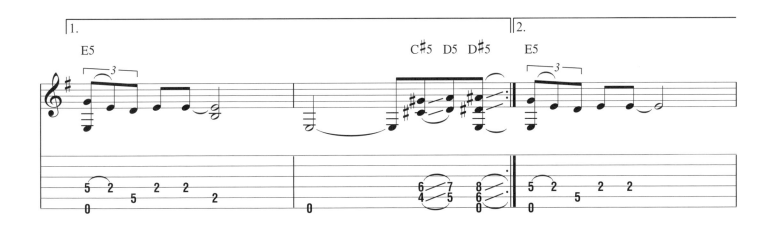

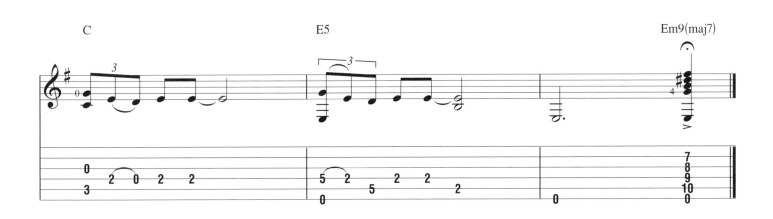

Quiet Nights of Quiet Stars
(Corcovado)

English Words by Gene Lees
Original Words and Music by Antonio Carlos Jobim

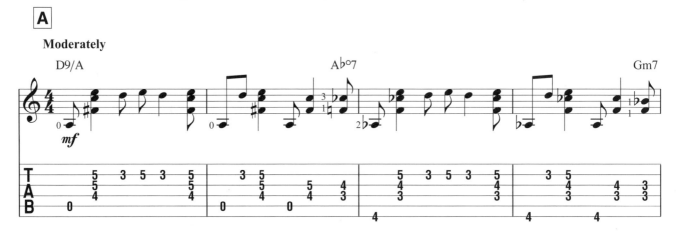

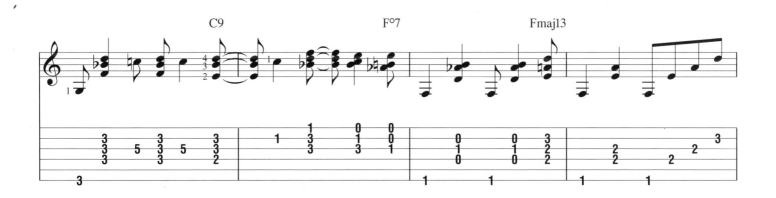

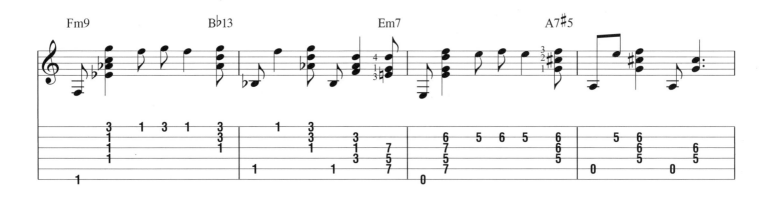

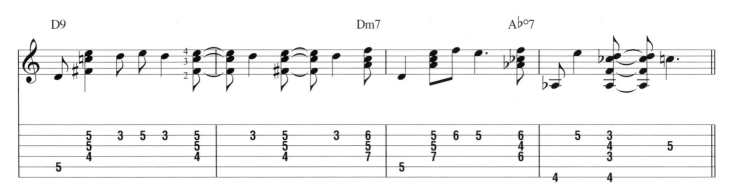

Copyright © 1962, 1964 ANTONIO CARLOS JOBIM
Copyright Renewed
This arrangement Copyright © 2009 ANTONIO CARLOS JOBIM
All Rights for English Speaking Countries Controlled and Administered by SONGS OF UNIVERSAL, INC.
All Rights Reserved   Used by Permission

'Round Midnight

Words by Bernie Hanighen
Music by Thelonious Monk and Cootie Williams

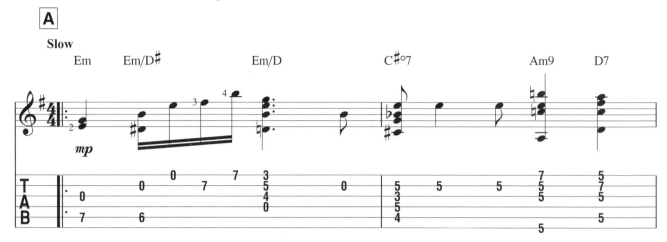

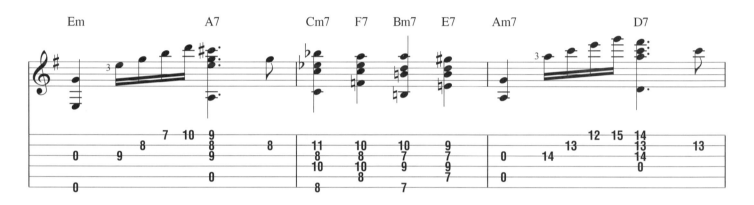

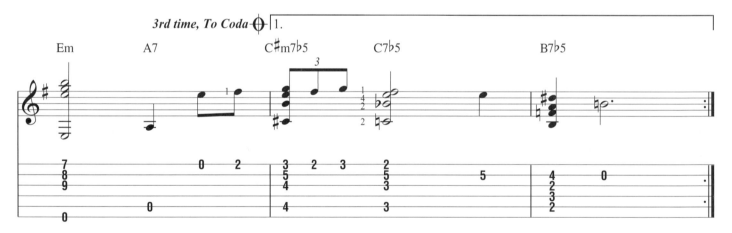

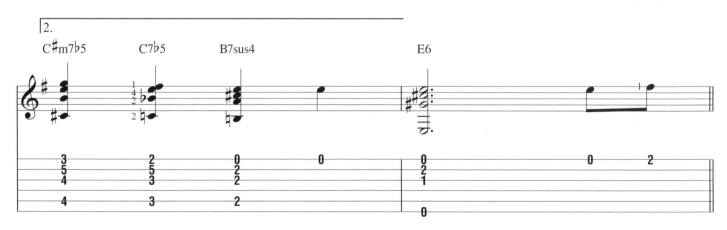

Copyright © 1944 (Renewed 1971) by Thelonious Music Corp. and WB Music Corp.
This arrangement Copyright © 2019 by Thelonious Music Corp. and WB Music Corp.
International Copyright Secured   All Rights Reserved

B

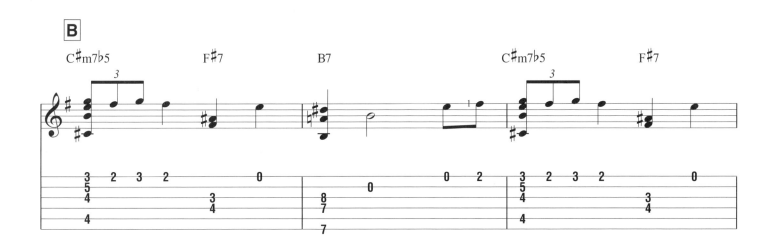

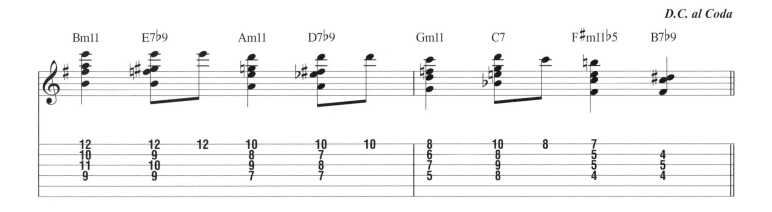

D.C. al Coda

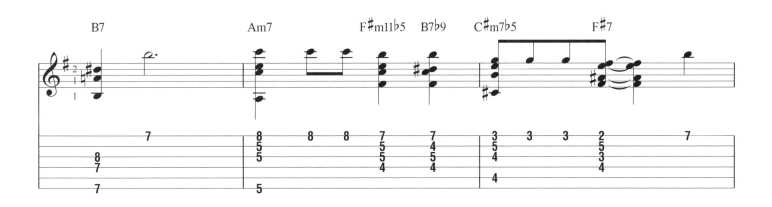

Coda

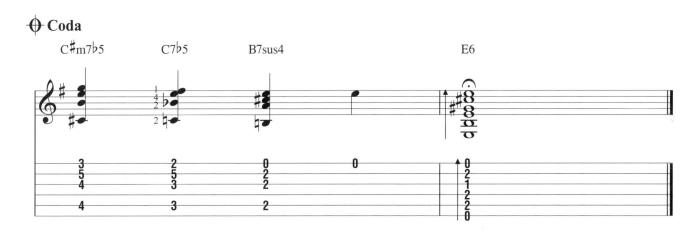

She's Got a Way

Words and Music by Billy Joel

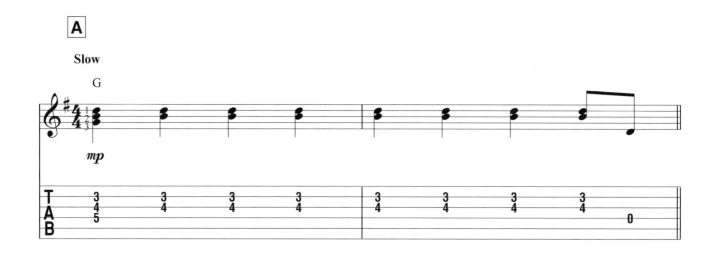

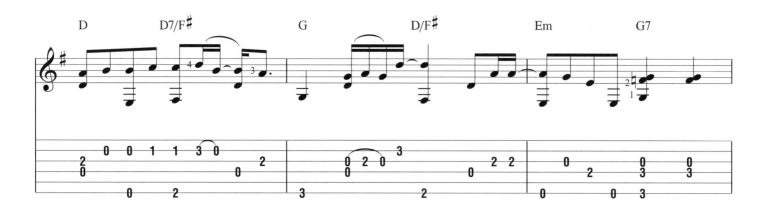

Copyright © 1971 IMPULSIVE MUSIC
Copyright Renewed
This arrangement Copyright © 2019 IMPULSIVE MUSIC
All Rights Administered by ALMO MUSIC CORP.
All Rights Reserved   Used by Permission

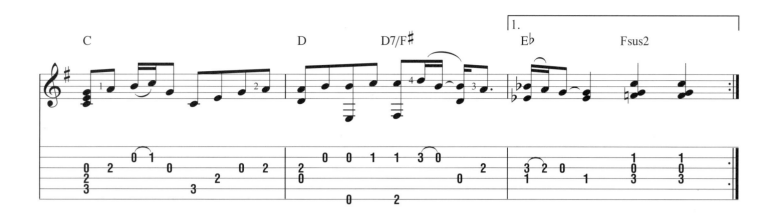

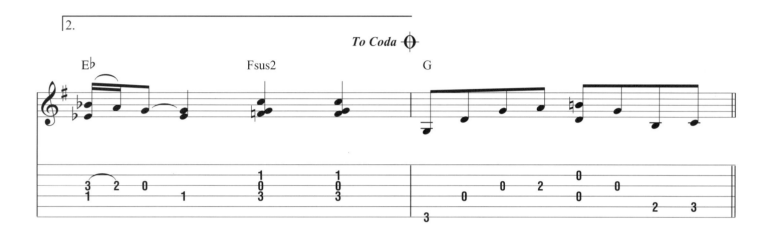

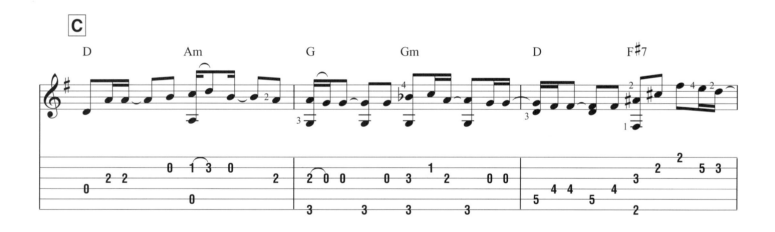

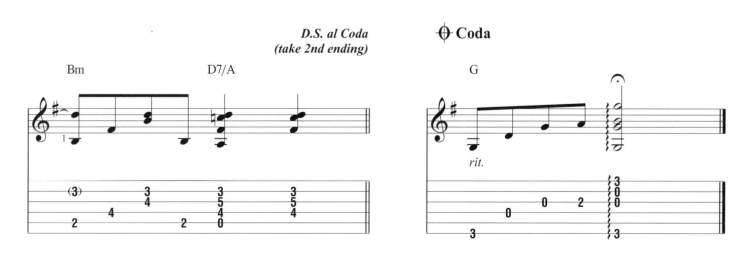

Songbird

Words and Music by Christine McVie

Copyright © 1977 by Universal Music - Careers
Copyright Renewed
This arrangement Copyright © 2019 by Universal Music - Careers
International Copyright Secured   All Rights Reserved

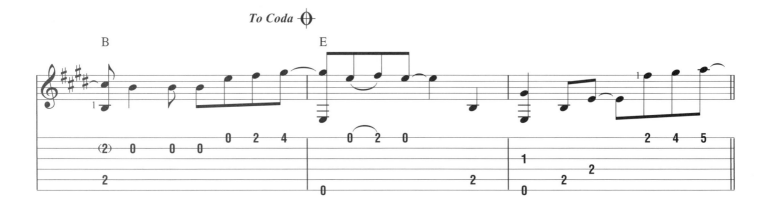

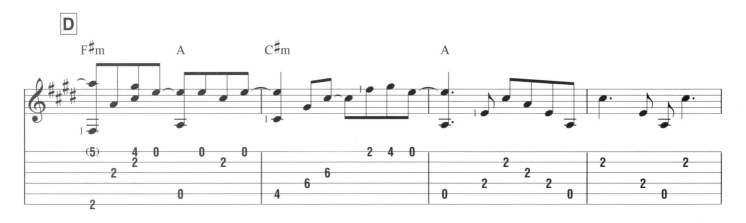

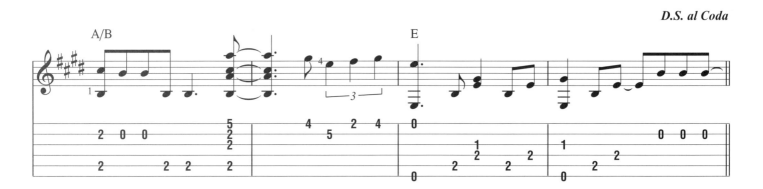

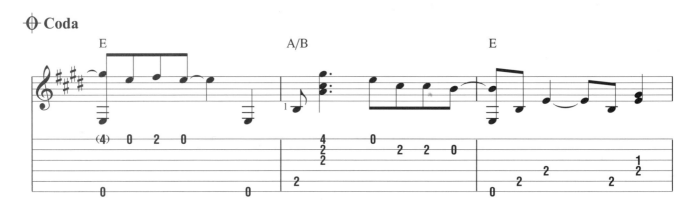

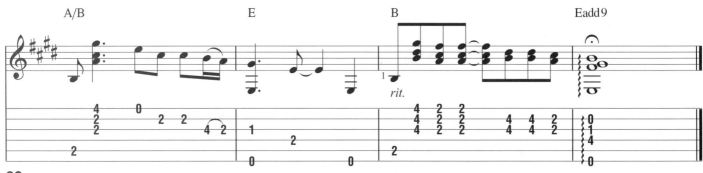

98

Sway
(Quien Será)

English Words by Norman Gimbel
Spanish Words and Music by Pablo Beltran Ruiz and Luis Demetrio Traconis Molina

Copyright © 1954 by Editorial Mexicana De Musica Internacional, S.A. and Words West LLC (P.O. Box 15187, Beverly Hills, CA 90209, USA)
Copyright Renewed
This arrangement Copyright © 2019 by Editorial Mexicana De Musica Internacional, S.A.
and Words West LLC (P.O. Box 15187, Beverly Hills, CA 90209, USA)
All Rights for Editorial Mexicana De Musica Internacional, S.A. Administered by Peer International Corporation
International Copyright Secured   All Rights Reserved

Stand by Me

Words and Music by Jerry Leiber, Mike Stoller and Ben E. King

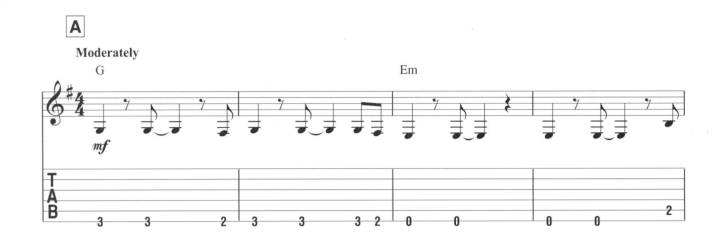

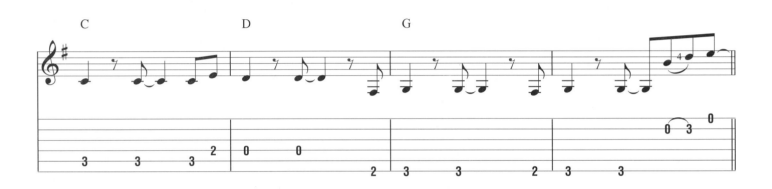

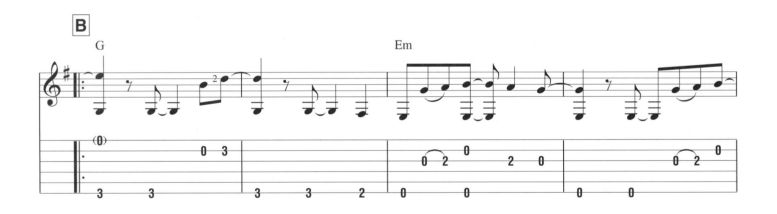

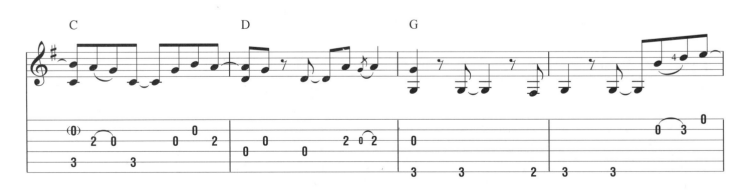

Copyright © 1961 Sony/ATV Music Publishing LLC
Copyright Renewed
This arrangement Copyright © 2019 Sony/ATV Music Publishing LLC
All Rights Administered by Sony/ATV Music Publishing LLC, 424 Church Street, Suite 1200, Nashville, TN 37219
International Copyright Secured   All Rights Reserved

Sunrise, Sunset

from the Musical FIDDLER ON THE ROOF

Words by Sheldon Harnick
Music by Jerry Bock

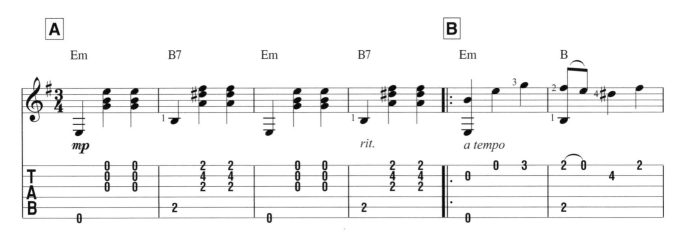

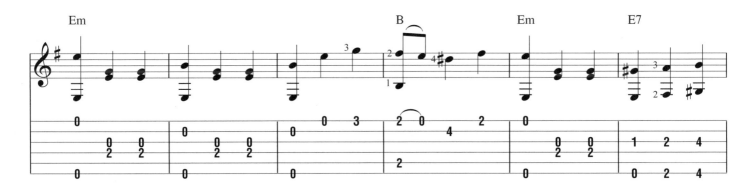

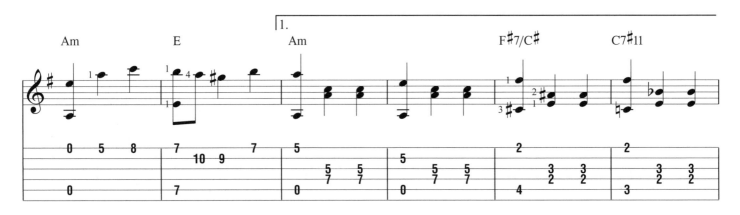

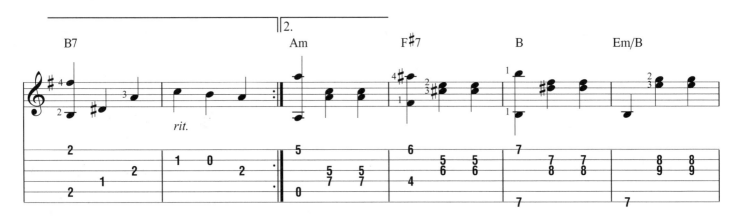

Copyright © 1964 Bock IP LLC and Mayerling Productions, Ltd.
Copyright Renewed 1992
This arrangement Copyright © 2019 Bock IP LLC and Mayerling Productions, Ltd.
All Rights for Mayerling Productions, Ltd. Administered by R&H Music, a Division of Rodgers & Hammerstein: an Imagem Company
International Copyright Secured   All Rights Reserved

Thinking Out Loud

Words and Music by Ed Sheeran and Amy Wadge

Copyright © 2014 Sony/ATV Music Publishing (UK) Limited and BDI Music Ltd.
This arrangement Copyright © 2019 Sony/ATV Music Publishing (UK) Limited and BDI Music Ltd.
All Rights on behalf of Sony/ATV Music Publishing (UK) Limited Administered by
Sony/ATV Music Publishing LLC, 424 Church Street, Suite 1200, Nashville, TN 37219
International Copyright Secured   All Rights Reserved

With or Without You

Words and Music by U2

Copyright © 1987 UNIVERSAL MUSIC PUBLISHING INTERNATIONAL B.V.
This arrangement Copyright © 2019 UNIVERSAL MUSIC PUBLISHING INTERNATIONAL B.V.
All Rights in the United States and Canada Controlled and Administered by UNIVERSAL - POLYGRAM INTERNATIONAL PUBLISHING, INC.
All Rights Reserved   Used by Permission

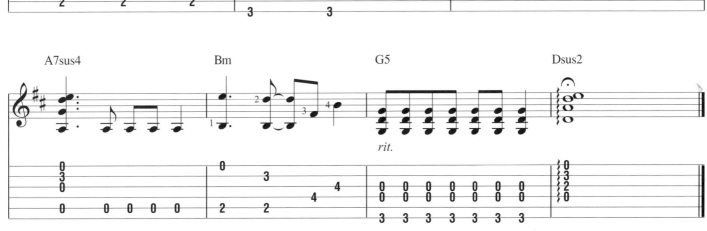

Time After Time

Words and Music by Cyndi Lauper and Rob Hyman

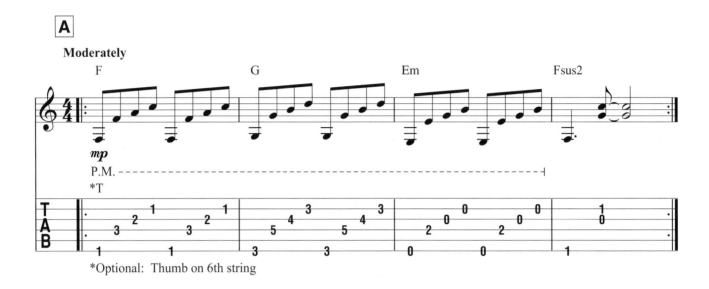

*Optional: Thumb on 6th string

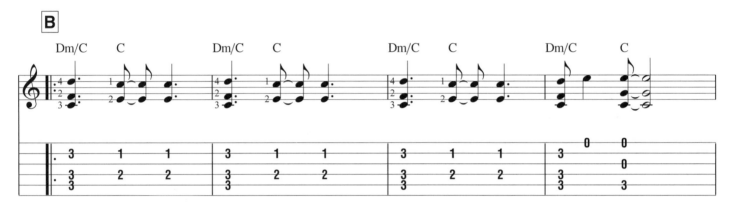

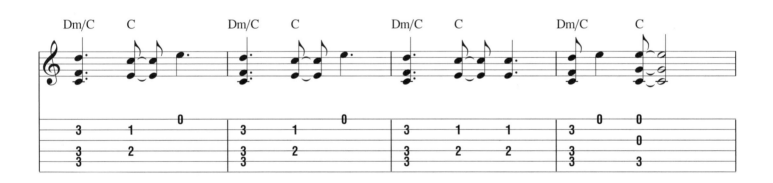

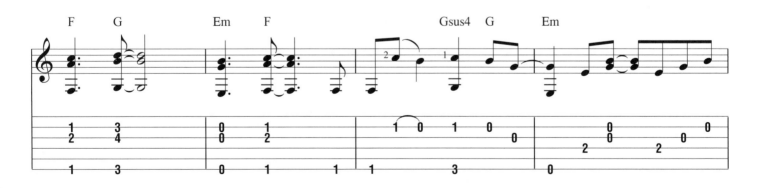

Copyright © 1983 Rellla Music Co. and Dub Notes
This arrangement Copyright © 2019 Rellla Music Co. and Dub Notes
All Rights for Rellla Music Co. Administered by Sony/ATV Music Publishing LLC, 424 Church Street, Suite 1200, Nashville, TN 37219
All Rights for Dub Notes Administered by WB Music Corp.
International Copyright Secured   All Rights Reserved

What a Wonderful World

Words and Music by George David Weiss and Bob Thiele

Copyright © 1967 by Range Road Music Inc., Quartet Music and Abilene Music
Copyright Renewed
This arrangement Copyright © 2019 by Range Road Music Inc., Quartet Music and Abilene Music, Inc.
All Rights for Range Road Music Inc. Administered by Round Hill Carlin, LLC
All Rights for Quartet Music Administered by BMG Rights Management (US) LLC
All Rights for Abilene Music Administered by Concord Sounds c/o Concord Music Publishing
International Copyright Secured   All Rights Reserved
Used by Permission

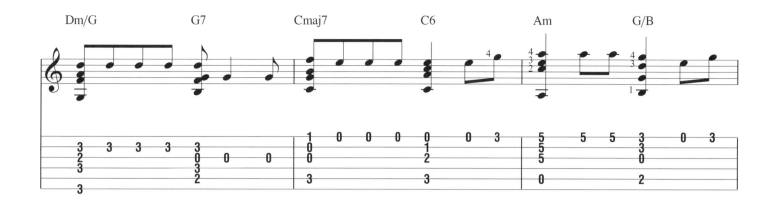

D.S. al Coda

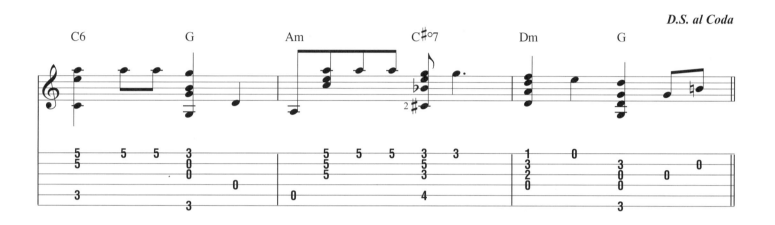

Coda

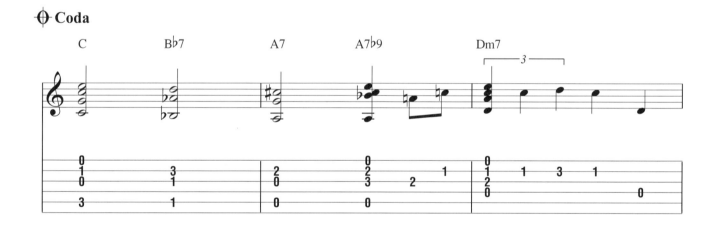

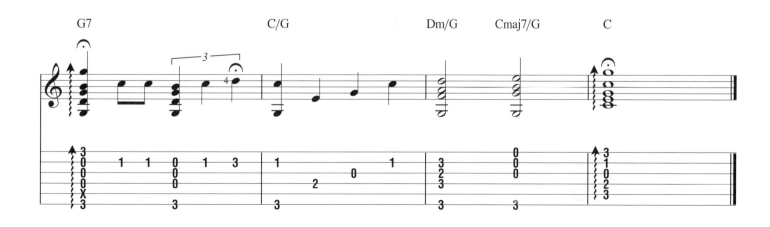

113

Wonderful Tonight

Words and Music by Eric Clapton

Copyright © 1977 by Eric Patrick Clapton
Copyright Renewed
This arrangement Copyright © 2019 by Eric Patrick Clapton
International Copyright Secured   All Rights Reserved

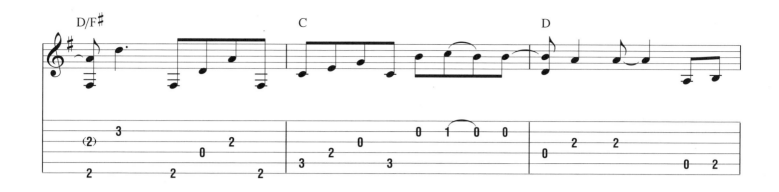

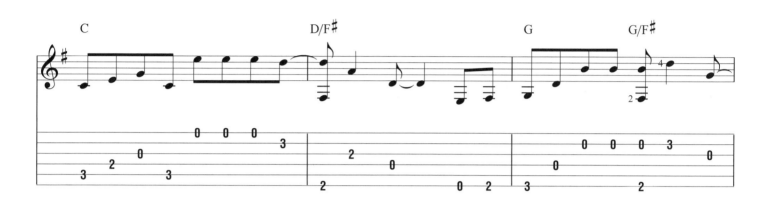

To Coda ⊕

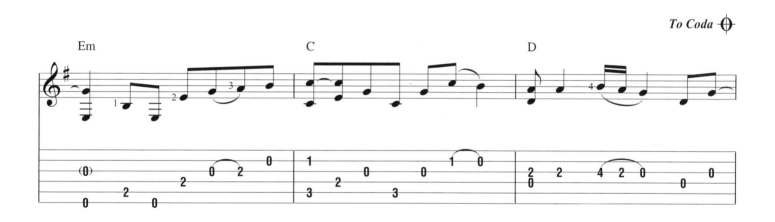

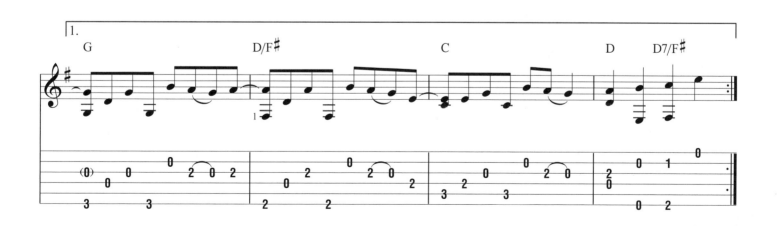

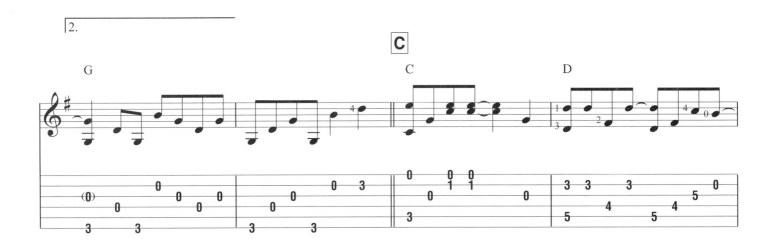

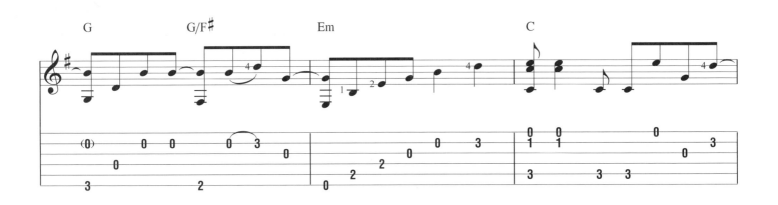

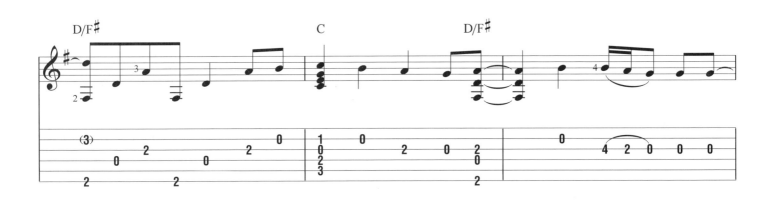

D.S. al Coda

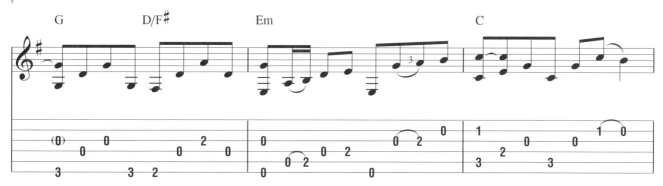

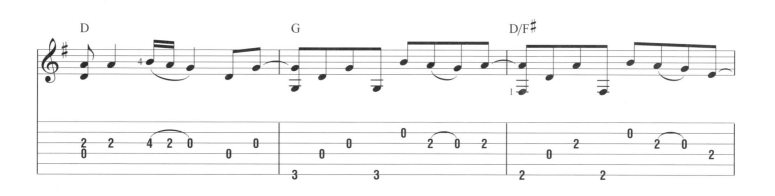

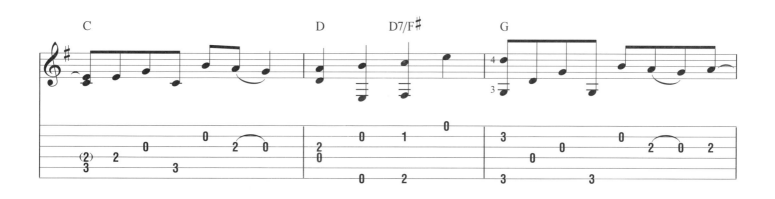

Yesterday

Words and Music by John Lennon and Paul McCartney

Copyright © 1965 Sony/ATV Music Publishing LLC
Copyright Renewed
This arrangement Copyright © 2019 Sony/ATV Music Publishing LLC
All Rights Administered by Sony/ATV Music Publishing LLC, 424 Church Street, Suite 1200, Nashville, TN 37219
International Copyright Secured   All Rights Reserved

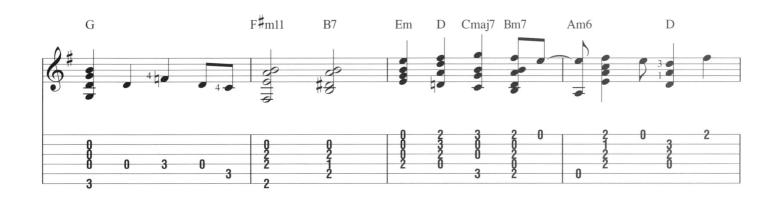

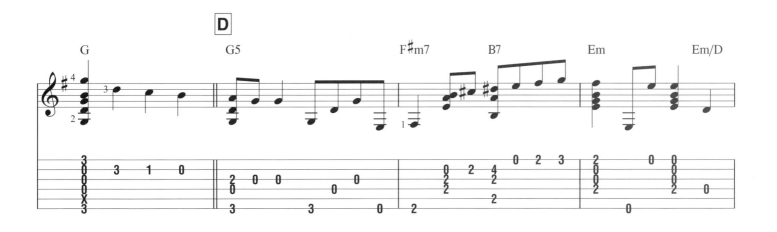

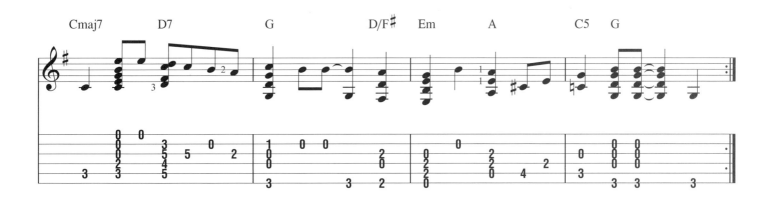

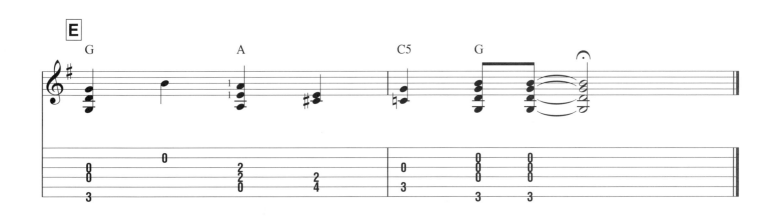

You Are So Beautiful

Words and Music by Billy Preston and Bruce Fisher

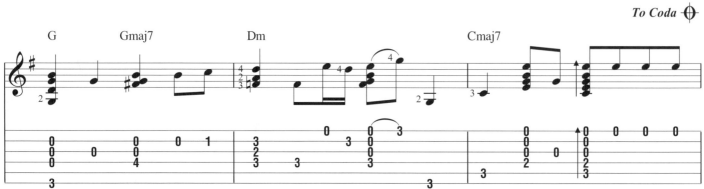

Copyright © 1973 IRVING MUSIC, INC. and ALMO MUSIC CORP.
Copyright Renewed
This arrangement Copyright © 2019 IRVING MUSIC, INC. and ALMO MUSIC CORP.
All Rights Reserved   Used by Permission

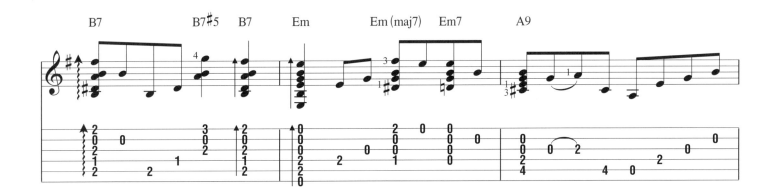

D.S. al Coda

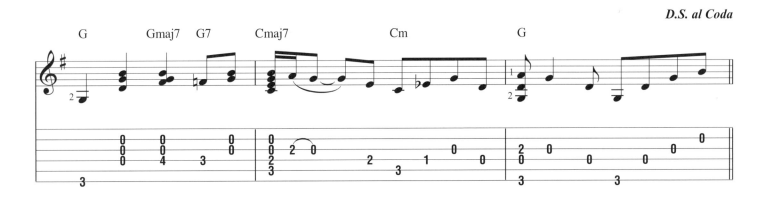

⊕ Coda

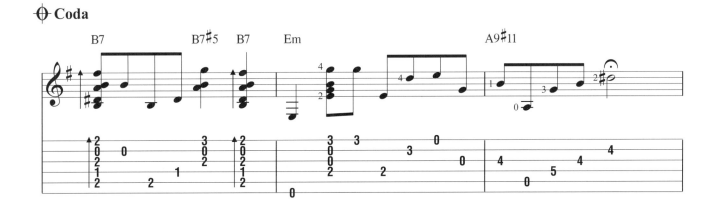

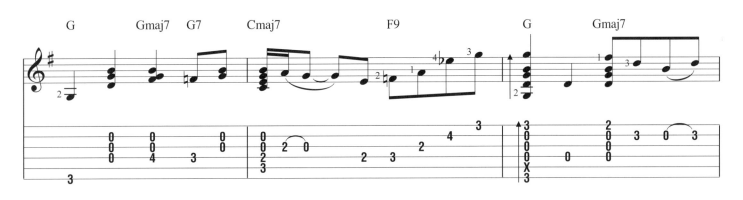

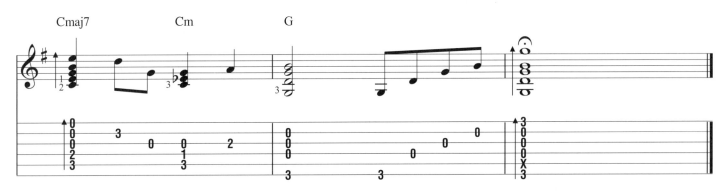

You Raise Me Up

Words and Music by Brendan Graham and Rolf Lovland

Copyright © 2002 by Peermusic (UK) Ltd. and Universal Music Publishing, A Division of Universal Music AS
This arrangement Copyright © 2019 by Peermusic (UK) Ltd. and Universal Music Publishing, A Division of Universal Music AS
All Rights for Peermusic (UK) Ltd. in the United States Controlled and Administered by Peermusic III, Ltd.
All Rights for Universal Music Publishing, A Division of Universal Music AS in the United States and Canada
Controlled and Administered by Universal - PolyGram International Publishing, Inc. (Publishing) and Alfred Music (Print)
International Copyright Secured   All Rights Reserved

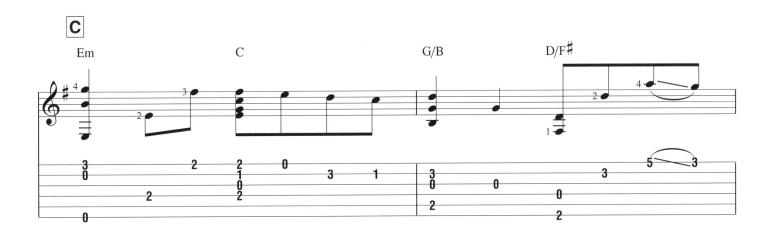

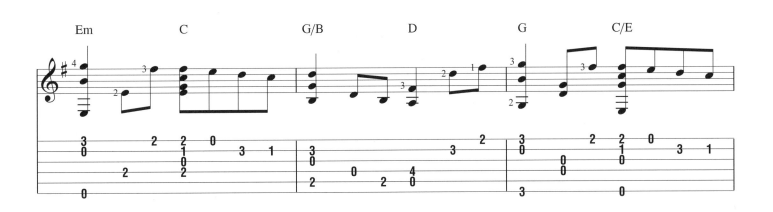

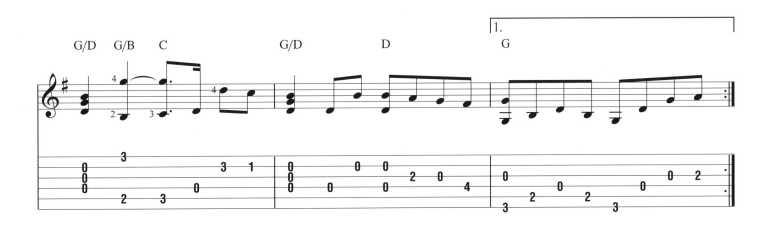

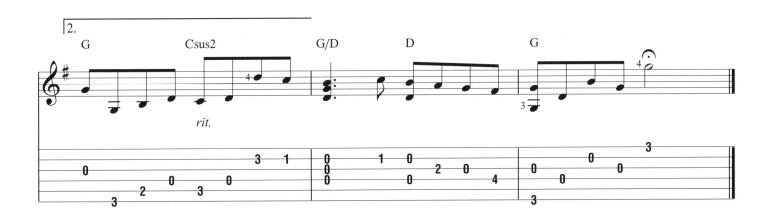

Your Song

Words and Music by Elton John and Bernie Taupin

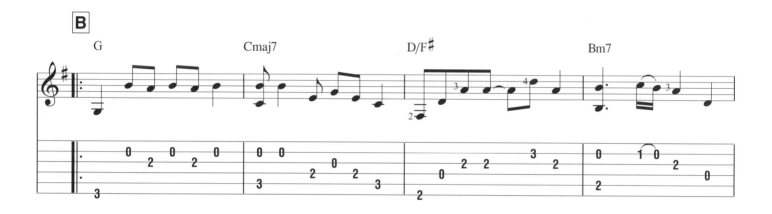

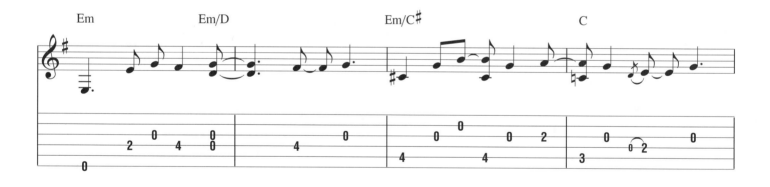

Copyright © 1969 UNIVERSAL/DICK JAMES MUSIC LTD.
Copyright Renewed
This arrangement Copyright © 2019 UNIVERSAL/DICK JAMES MUSIC LTD.
All Rights in the United States and Canada Controlled and Administered by UNIVERSAL - SONGS OF POLYGRAM INTERNATIONAL, INC.
All Rights Reserved   Used by Permission

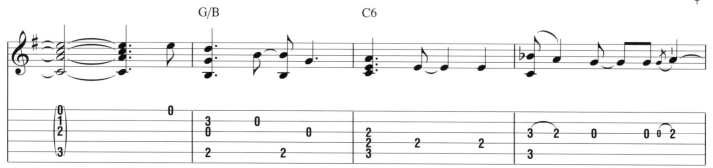

D.C. al Coda
(take repeat)

$\oplus$ **Coda**

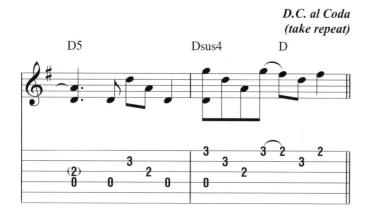

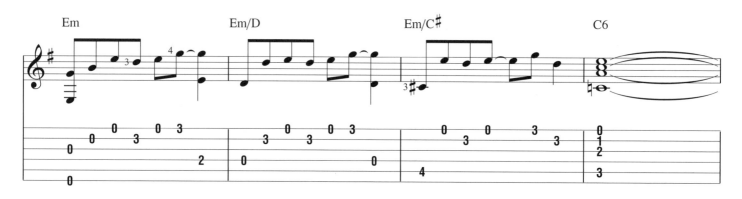

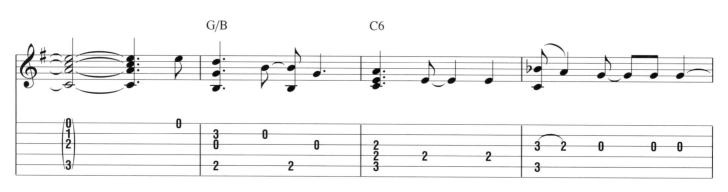

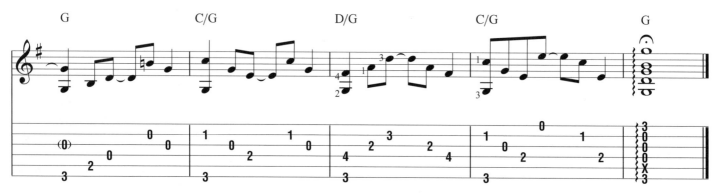